Troubled Children/ Troubled Parents: The Way Out
2nd Edition

Also by Stanley Goldstein

Nonfiction
Shopping For A Shrink:
Finding the Right Psychotherapist For You or Your
Child
Sound Advice and Stories to Change Your Life

Fiction
Lies In Progress

Park West:
A Novel of Love and Murder and Redemption

Ghosts and Angels: A Memoir
How, During an Epoch of Terror, Goodness Vanquished
Evil and Restored Faith

STANLEY GOLDSTEIN

TROUBLED CHILDREN/ TROUBLED PARENTS: THE WAY OUT 2nd EDITION

WYSTON BOOKS, INC.

WYSTON BOOKS, INC.
P.O. Box 1280
Warwick, NY 10990-1280

Tel.: (845) 986-6888
E-mail: askus@wystonbooks.com
Please visit our website: www.wystonbooks.com

Goldstein, Stanley
Troubled Children/Troubled Parents: The Way Out
2nd Edition
Includes bibliographical references
1. Emotional problems of children
2. Parent and child
3. Mentally ill children
1. Child psychotherapy—Residential treatment

Troubled Children/Troubled Parents: The Way Out
1st Edition was published by Atheneum (New York City)

Library of Congress Control Number: 2010942834

ISBN 978-0-9717705-8-4 (print edition)
ISBN 978-0-9717705-9-1 (E-book edition)

Cover photograph by Paul Viant/
Photographers Choice RF Collection
Licensed from Getty Images

To My Patients

The author is grateful to the following for permission to reproduce brief passages:

To *The American Journal of Orthopsychiatry* and Lee Coleman, M.D., for a passage from his paper "Problem Kids and Preventive Medicine: The Making of an Odd Couple." Reprinted, with permission, from *The American Journal of Orthopsychiatry*. Copyright © 1978 by The American Orthopsychiatry Association, Inc.

To Jason Aronson, Inc., for a passage from *Mental Health and Law* by Alan A. Stone, M.D. Copyright © 1976.

To Basic Books, Inc. (New York City), and The Hogarth Press Ltd. (London) for a passage from Paper 29, "Recommendations for Physicians on the Psycho-Analytic Method of Treatment," in *The Collected Papers of Sigmund Freud,* vol. 2, edited by Ernest Jones, M.D., authorized translation under the supervision of Joan Riviere, published by Basic Books, Inc., Publishers, New York, by arrangement with The Hogarth Press Ltd. and The Institute of Psycho-analysis, London.

To The New American Library, Inc., for a passage from Sophocles' *Antigone* in *The Oedipus Plays of Sophocles*, translated by Paul Roche. Copyright © 1958.

To W. W. Norton & Co., Inc., for a passage from *Faust*, translated by Walter Arndt, edited by Cyrus Hamlin. Copyright © 1976.

To The Princeton University Press for a passage from *Racine's Mid-Career Tragedies*, translated into English with Introductions by Lacy Lockert. Copyright © 1959 by The Princeton University Press. Reprinted by permission of The Princeton University Press.

To The University of Chicago Press for a passage from Sophocles' *Ajax*, translated by John Moore, edited by David Grene and Richmond Lattimore. Copyright © 1957 by The University of Chicago.

Identifying characteristics not essential to understanding the condition and course of treatment of patients described in this work have been changed to assure their anonymity.

Every time that we accuse and judge,
we have not reached the ground.

—Paul Valéry

AUTHOR'S PREFACE TO
THE 1ST EDITION
How This Book Came to Be Written

I had not planned to write exactly this book. The book my contract required was a slimmer one describing only those techniques I had discovered over the years to be most effective in helping children when they are troubled, in healing them when they are in pain. But before the contract negotiations were yet completed I knew that the book would include other matters: my experiences over the years, most particularly at The Hospital, a major treatment setting which, for obvious reasons, must remain nameless.

A colleague at The Hospital, sitting in a cafe while on vacation in Europe, suddenly began crying when she realized that she had to return to her job the next day. This was my frequent experience in those days when I was writing this book, even as I walked the streets of New York City, relaxing at free moments from my private practice.

I never cried during my years at The Hospital; now, years later, remembering those experiences, I cried. And out of those tears and those memories came a part of this book.

And so I ask the reader: Join me! Read about those difficulties which children naturally develop in the course of their life and those anxieties which parents naturally experience while interacting with them, and learn how the pain of both can be alleviated.

Learn how the more serious difficulties which children may develop arise and how they can be avoided. Learn how to be an effective parent when forced to cope with your children's problems.

Then read of the unhappiness experienced by adults when their childhood has gone awry. And share with me my memories, both painful and humorous. You will be changed as I have been.

I would like to extend the greatest of thanks to those who enabled me to have published, more quickly than I dared hope, this book which, being a combination of child guidance and narrative, fits within no traditional category:

To Harriet F. Pilpel, my literary agent.

To Judith T. Kern, my editor at Atheneum.

Finally (but certainly not least in importance), I would like to thank my sister, Myrna Siegel of Washington, D.C., who was ever willing, despite her family and professional responsibilities, to listen, with that confidentiality inculcated by her legal training and characteristic of our friendship, to the conversation of an author whose book was in process of gestation and who was thus unable, even while realizing how tiresome he was, to speak of other matters.

AUTHOR'S PREFACE TO THE 2nd EDITION

Re-reading a book that one has written is like attending a family reunion which went well. It is good to meet familiar people though it is sad that I never learned how the lives of these people have changed.

In the thirty years since *Troubled Children/Troubled Parents* was first published, embarrassingly little of significance has occurred in the treatment of mental health. Widely publicized research on medications and genetics appear—only to disappear without comment a few months later. Perhaps the most important advance in the healing of formerly untreatable disorders was provided by James F. Masterson, M.D., a psychoanalyst who died in 2010. His popular book explaining his life's work, *The Search for the Real Self* (The Free Press/Macmillan, 1988), is well worth reading. Other crucial developments are the increase in observational studies of infants during their earliest months, revealing that, "in some ways, babies may be smarter, more thoughtful and more conscious than adults."* This research evidences the great importance of parenting in a child's healthy emotional development. Anecdotal evidence of this can be gained from Stacy's story in Chapter Eleven. It aroused my tears and may produce yours.

Though being of retirement age I'm still in practice, having discovered no other professional activity apart from writing which is as enjoyable—and valuable! Perhaps the following story will explain why.

A six year old, very anxious girl sat in my waiting room while I spoke with her mother. There, she met a child who wasn't a patient and who she knew from school. He asked her, "What are you doing here?" "I have scary dreams," she replied. The boy responded, "I have scary dreams too. Maybe I should talk to him." And, soon, her scary dreams vanished.

Comments are, as always, welcome.

Stanley Goldstein, Ph.D.
New York City – Hudson Valley, New York
May, 1978 – January, 2011

E-mail: drstan@drstanleygoldstein.com
www.drstanleygoldstein.com

*"Awakening the child inside," *The Monitor on Psychology,* January 2011, 42, 1, p.34

Contents

Part One: Of Unhappy Children and Uneasy Parents

Part Two: Of Children and Their Doctors at The Hospital

PART ONE

*Of Unhappy Children
& Uneasy Parents*

INTRODUCTION

Troubled Children, Troubled Parents: The Way Out

Many years before I would have regarded her mother's description of Joan's behavior as improbable. But that day I accepted the report as being accurate. My psychotherapeutic experience with countless children and adolescents had taught me never to dismiss any description of a child's behavior no matter how unbelievable it might initially seem. Over the years, through contact with my patients, my concept of children, their capacities and emotions, had broadened. I had, for example, met Kathy, a precocious 41/2 -year-old girl who was more seductive than any adult woman I had ever encountered. And I had met Robert, an intelligent adolescent boy who as a young child had been diagnosed as "autistic" and, ten years later, spent his days speaking of clocks and watches and electric motors. So when I met Joan, I believed her mother's story.

Joan was a tall, thin, seven-year-old. Her mother had brought her to my office in desperation: Joan was about to be expelled from school! Her behavior in class was so defiant and difficult to contain that most of her school days were spent in the principal's office. He had even joked that a special annex should be constructed next to his office for Joan so rarely was she in class. Yet within two months of her initial appointment with me, Joan's behavior had changed radically. Now she was sent to the principal so rarely that, one day, he made a special visit to Joan's classroom to see if she was still attending school.

How had I helped Joan? How had my actions been so "catalytic" that she was set free from her unhappiness and could participate with interest and pleasure in her academic and social school experiences? I used no esoteric or highly specialized technique; nor could my interaction with Joan be considered "behavior modification" in the strictest sense, even though a modification in her behavior was certainly the result. Instead, I observed and I listened for certain behavior and speech, and I spoke in a particular manner.

Several years later I spoke with Carla, the divorced mother of two young children. She was concerned over the recent behavior of her younger (six-year-old) son. After spending a rare afternoon with his father (who lived fifteen hundred miles away from his children), the boy locked himself in his room and refused to allow his mother admittance. She stood outside the door, listening, as he berated and slapped his favorite stuffed animal. He condemned the animal for its behavior, and vowed to have no more to do with it.

Carla's anxiety rose as she listened to her son's angry voice. She again requested that he open the door and again she was ignored. Her son's loud condemnation of his animal continued for some time. Then there was silence. The door opened and her son, wordlessly, walked out of the room clutching his animal. He would not explain the behavior which had so puzzled and troubled his mother. His behavior during the remainder of the week was unexceptional.

When I spoke with Carla I explained the frightening incident as I understood it. I said that her son was very angry. Having had no direct contact with the boy, I would not presume to state the source of his anger. It may have reflected his perceived abandonment by his father or his own feeling of guilt over the break-up of his family. It may have reflected his discontent over a specific event which had occurred that afternoon. I could not be sure. But in those moments when he was alone in his room berating his stuffed animal, he was resolving his unhappiness. The anger he was verbalizing was analogous to the pus pouring out of a physical wound: he was healing himself. When he opened the door of his room he had no need to discuss this incident with his mother: the "wound" was healed and so he could go on about his life.

Carla was greatly relieved by my explanation. She had been concerned for days that her son's behavior reflected both the child's serious emotional difficulty and her own inadequacy as a mother; she thought that such troubles might be an unavoidable consequence of her attempt to function as both parents in her single-parent family. How had I succeeded in comforting Carla? My information gave her no additional facts about her son: indeed, it was she who provided me with such facts as there were. What I did was to provide her with a perspective on child development and child behavior different from her own. It was this perspective—not any required change in her child—which comforted her.

Through my years of experience as a psychologist, in my work with both seriously troubled and essentially healthy children, I have shared this perspective with many parents. It is because of the comfort and understanding which my professional knowledge has provided these parents that I write this book. My purpose is to enable parents to interact with their child when they are troubled in such a way as to provide them with understanding, comfort, and healing.

The most potent factor in the reduction of anxiety is understanding. Through a proper understanding of the difficulties which children naturally experience in the course of their development, much of the anxiety experienced by both children and parents can be reduced. But it is not only for the normally experienced, "typical" problems of youth that helpful, anxiety-reducing parental intervention can be useful. There are ways of understanding and relating to even the most severely disturbed child that can do much to comfort both parent and child. To be able to help children when they are troubled one must acquire certain facts and techniques and forget other largely inaccurate information about ways of relating to children. Each person—parent and child—may be considered to be a psychologist of sorts, for every individual in the course of their life has studied their own behavior and that of others and from this study has derived certain conclusions about human development. Indeed, one noted psychologist, Fritz Heider, spent much of his career compiling a "naive psychology," the term he coined for the conclusions about human behavior which a person naturally acquires in the course of their life.'

For example, one "fact" of this naive psychology is that children differ from adults because they possess less factual information than adults. However as we will see in Chapter 3, this conclusion, while accurate, is far and away the least important distinction between the intellectual capacities of children and those of adults (or a child and their parents).

Another "rule" derived from naive psychology, and used frequently by both children and adults, is that decisions (and therefore behavior) are based upon information derived from the environment. For example, if we believe that one's primary source of information is visual, then our desire to remain inconspicuous—to hide—when unpleasant chores are being handed out becomes easily understandable.

The task of a psychologist, I think, is far easier than that of a parent. I have often reflected, in my work with parents, on the severe emotional demands which parenting even a "normal" child presents although these demands are far less than those one encounters when attempting to interact with a child who is troubled. There are few children with whom I work in my clinical practice that I could tolerate living with on a permanent basis. Yet I have feelings of compassion and warmth for all of these children and a sense of optimism about the possibility of positive change in their lives.

Some years ago I spoke with a divorced woman in her late thirties and her ten-year-old son. Her son had very serious emotional difficulties: although his physical and intellectual capabilities were equal to those of his peers, his emotional development lagged far behind. He was most immature: a four-year-old child would be ashamed to behave in such a nagging, overdependent fashion. But no four-year-old would have knowledge of the obscenities with which this child continually expressed himself. His mother said that, at times, she hated her son. But her psychotherapist had admonished her that her duty as a mother was to like her child, that her anger toward him was "immature." I told her that while I could feel compassion toward her son, I could see nothing likable in his behavior; and, in my opinion, her therapist's criticism reflected his lack of knowledge (for he treated only adults) of the great discomfort which the behavior of a severely troubled child could cause a family.

I once treated, in a hospital, a severely disturbed adolescent: some evidence existed that he had been involved, at the age of four, in the death of his father. Whether or not this accusation was valid, he had been accused of it by his mother for many years. At the age of seven he hanged the family dog. In later years he removed the steps from the staircase of his home, stole money, and destroyed property. When I began treating him he was extraordinarily provocative and controlling. Often he would push his way into my office and refuse to leave. At times he would grab my telephone and make random calls. At other times he would steal papers from my desk, but returned them several hours later. His great height and weight made it very difficult to set appropriate limits and I became very angry at his behavior.

The significant change in him (and in our intense treatment relationship) began when one day, having reached the limits of my patience, I grabbed him and threw him out of my office (something he actually allowed me to do for had he wanted to resist, his size would have overwhelmed me). Three and one-half years later this boy was greatly changed. He functioned superbly in a vocational training program where his friendly attitude and outstanding sense of responsibility made him an excellent worker. Had I a business, I would not have hesitated to hire him.

I cannot imagine any advice more destructive than to tell parents to be continually accepting toward their child's behavior regardless of its measure of civility.

I ask you, the reader, to join with me in a mutual exploration of how one can most helpfully relate to the behavior of children when they are troubled. I have found that only rarely do the goals of those children and adolescents with whom I work professionally differ from the goals desired for them by their parents. These are, generally, the capacity to be independent, the capacities for friendship, emotional warmth, and love, and the capacity to feel comfortable with oneself. Surely few can disagree with goals such as these. Thus our task here will be to consider certain facts and to explore certain techniques that will make you as parents better able to help your children achieve these goals. And as you gain this increased ability to interact with them, it is inevitable that, in the process, you will also learn more about yourselves and thereby be better able to help your children achieve those goals.

Notes

1. Fritz Heider, *The Psychology of Interpersonal Relations* (New York City: Wiley, 1958).

CHAPTER ONE

And the Suffering Goes Unnoticed...

The emotional capacities of children are frequently undervalued by adults: it is believed that they feel less deeply than adults and have a less complete repertoire of emotions. Yet a research study performed more than thirty-five years ago revealed that children as young as twenty-four months were capable of experiencing no fewer than ten separate emotions (affection, elation, joy, delight, excitement, distress, jealousy, anger, disgust, and fear).[1] Considering the number of parents who hold this inaccurate view of their children's emotional capacities, it is little wonder that there is so great a demand for mental health services among our adult population. Emotional difficulties which develop and remain un-healed in childhood become more serious and difficult to remedy with each passing year.

The Woman's Collection: A Razor and Pills and Rope

Some years ago I was associated with a major mental health facility for children in the Midwest. On the staff of that clinic was an extraordinarily gifted child therapist, Dr. B. His skill in treating the most severely disturbed children was legendary. On occasion he also served as a consultant to adults with equally severe disorders.

One day he agreed, as a favor to a colleague, to meet with a woman for several sessions only (for his work schedule was really filled). The woman came into his office and told him about her life. She was in her mid-thirties and had experienced immense emotional suffering since her earliest childhood. She spoke of her extensive efforts to remedy her difficulties: years of psychotherapy with countless practitioners, innumerable medications, electroconvulsive shock therapy, insulin shock therapy, all to no avail. Her life remained one of insufferable misery, totally lacking in warmth and social contact. So she decided to end her life, and came to Dr. B. to share with him the agony of her existence, to seek from him one reason why she should not commit suicide.

Dr. B. had no doubt of the accuracy of the woman's description of her life; nor did he doubt that she intended to carry out her suicide upon leaving his office. And so he spoke to her simply, and with great care. He said, "You have suffered greatly in your life. I would not tell you that you must continue to live, for such a commitment belongs to each individual alone. But I am not convinced that significant change cannot be effected in your life. If you will work with me and I come to believe that this is not true, that your suffering cannot be relieved, then I will obtain for you whatever drug you may desire to end your life so that you can finally achieve the peace you deserve."

The woman agreed to continue to see Dr. B., who found room for her in his impossibly busy schedule. On her next visit she brought to him for safekeeping those objects which were capable of causing her death and she had collected over the years: pills of various types, a razor, and a rope. Dr. B. put them into his desk drawer and said that if the day came when she wished their return he would give them to her.

The woman and Dr. B. collaborated for several years, and there was some positive change in her life. But the day came when she felt that she could no longer endure her suffering. And so she asked Dr. B. for her objects, the razor and pills and rope which he had been holding for her. Dr. B. returned them. When she left his office he wept. Several days later the woman telephoned and entered into treatment with him once again. In the ensuing weeks they realized that her recently intensified desire to kill herself was a reaction against her growing realization that her life, unhappy though it was, had, through the caring and commitment of another person (Dr. B.), finally acquired a sense of meaning.

The suffering which this woman endured was extraordinary; had effective professional help been provided early in her childhood, there is little doubt that her years of agony could have been avoided. Yet as illustrative as this story is of the possibility of change even in cases of the most severe psychological difficulties, its drama perhaps too effectively tends to conceal a simple but important message: that, whether in child or adult, even the most frightening and bizarre behavior and speech derive from simple unmet human needs. Had this woman's needs been satisfied as a child, her needs for warmth and open communication and emotional support (among others), the story of her life would have been far different.

Much as it is difficult to conceive of a blazing fire as having derived from the sparks which ignited it, so too it is difficult to conceive of the sometimes complex, often dramatic difficulties which children can develop as deriving from the misunderstandings and misconceptions which occurred years before, and often between the best intentioned parents and their children. Before learning the techniques for alleviating these difficulties before they become serious, it would be useful to consider what children experience when they are troubled.

Tom, an adult suffering almost crippling psychological difficulties, told the following story about his isolated early childhood. When he was four years old he felt very alone in his family. His parents were unhappily married and, although concerned with his welfare, were incapable of divorcing themselves from their own personal conflicts in order to be able to give emotionally to their child. As Tom's discomfort in the family setting increased, so did the fears which symbolized it. One day, as he was throwing a ball in the street, it rolled into the darkened cellar of an apartment house. He went into the cellar to retrieve it and there met two maintenance men. "Humorously" they told Tom to beware of the "wild animals" that lurked there. Tom grabbed his ball and dashed from the cellar.

Soon afterward he began to be afraid to enter darkened rooms alone. Several months later his grandmother took him to see the revival of an early German film classic, *M*. Its story concerns the crime and punishment of a child murderer. Tom experienced no fear at the time but in later weeks he became obsessed with the frightening belief that there lived in the sewer a horrifying man, a black-clothed strangler, who waited for him in dark corners and from whom he could never be safe. Tom didn't speak of these fears until fifteen years later, when he revealed them in the course of his psychotherapy.

To be a helpful parent one must at times adopt a scientific attitude. But this attitude is different from the emotionally constricted, unfeeling stereotype which many believe to be scientific. Rather, a scientist's attitude may be described as their impassioned quest for valid conclusions after first collecting data through accurate observations. Thus it is not surprising that Jean Piaget, one of the most brilliant child psychologists of the twentieth century, has suggested that it is affect (feeling) which provides the force motivating all intellectual activity.[2] What can we, using a scientific attitude, conclude about the emotional experience of a troubled child from the knowledge we now have about this four-year-old boy, Tom?

Emotions Experienced by a Child When They are Troubled

1. Our first conclusion would seem to be that a troubled child experiences considerable discomfort or, to use a psychological term, *anxiety*. Perhaps no word in recent years has been so overused with so little knowledge of its accurate definition as the term anxiety. Anxiety is simply a feeling (like love and sorrow and hate) which is unlike some other feelings in that it has distinctively unpleasant characteristics. These characteristics may be both physiological (a rapid heartbeat, stomach pains, trembling, increased sweating) and psychological (the intense fear of an imagined danger). Thus, when a child is troubled, whether mildly or seriously, they *feel bad*, much as they do when suffering from a physical ailment.

2. A troubled child is *afraid*. It is almost impossible for us to conceive of the kind of fear which Tom experienced as a child, fervently believing as he did that his life was endangered by wild animals and a horrifying strangler. Perhaps if we were to multiply by a factor of ten or so the fear we experience when we are walking alone down a deserted street at 3:00 A.M. and suddenly hear footsteps behind us, we could gain some awareness of the terror which Tom experienced.

3. A troubled child feels *powerless*. Tom was a small person (a child) in a world populated by larger, more capable beings (adults). He was physically unable to cope with the dangers confronting him and had no allies to whom he could turn for support. Can we wonder at Tom's feeling of helplessness?

4. A troubled child feels continually *tense*. Tom believed that his life was in danger: behind every shadow, in every darkened room, existed the possibility of menace. He had to be eternally vigilant, ready to act instantly to protect himself against the mortal dangers confronting him.

5. A troubled child is *preoccupied with his difficulties*. Because the "dangers" Tom confronted were so great (for he experienced them as being threats to his continued existence), it is no wonder that Tom had little involvement with others: his major interest could only be self-protection. He had no time for the interests which more naturally typify the life experience of young children (socialization, play, education).

6. A troubled child has *an unwavering belief in the reality of their difficulties*. Because Tom's imagined menace (ferocious animals, a strangler) symbolically represented the actual grave unhappiness which existed in his family setting, confronting the fantasy was less threatening than confronting that which it symbolized. A child is a helpless creature, totally dependent upon their parents (or parent surrogates) for the physical supports (food, shelter) and emotional nurturing which make both life and healthy development possible. Were he to be deprived of these supports, he literally could not survive. Thus a young child could more easily conceive of protecting themselves against a ferocious animal or a strange murderer than face the fact that they are essentially alone in the world, dependent upon parents who are uncaring and incapable of nurturing them.

7. A troubled child is *depressed*. One explanation of depression is that it is the feeling of one who is unable to achieve an important goal: thus they experience despair, give up, and reduce their interest in life. The most important goal for Tom was to protect himself from the menace which he believed enveloped him. Because his attempt was doomed to failure (for his real danger was other than what he believed it to be), there is every reason to suspect that he felt depressed.

In the previous pages we attempted to understand the emotional experience of a troubled child, to realize how the experience of being troubled feels. But before parents can intervene effectively in alleviating their child's unhappiness, they must first be able to recognize those subtle cues through which a troubled child solicits aid, those *Signals for Concern* through which they cry out for help. In the remainder of this chapter we will concern ourselves with these early signs of warning, the nine *Signals for Concern* through which a child attempts to communicate their unhappiness.

Virtually all readers of this book will have seen these "signals" in their own children. For despite the pronouncements of some clinicians, there do not exist two categories of children: untroubled (those who are happy and whose behavior can be readily understood) and troubled (those who are miserable and whose behavior is inexplicable). Rather, the behavior and level of satisfaction of children may be conceived as a continuum from the untroubled to the troubled, with all shades of gradation in between. And the same techniques which can be used for providing understanding and comfort to the psychologically healthy child when they, inevitably, become temporarily troubled, are appropriate to alleviate the almost continual suffering of the most troubled youth.

While these signals are those which all parents have observed in their own child's behavior, there are few parents—if my years of experience in treating troubled children and advising their parents is a valid indication—who can explain accurately either the meaning of these signals or the appropriate helpful response to the child who exhibits them.

The Nine Signals for Concern: Indicators of Distress in a Child

1. The first signal is a significant difference between the content of a child's statement and the depth of emotion they express.

    Children have preferences as do adults. What we are now concerned with are those instances in which the emotion expressed by the child far exceeds the frustration of the situation that confronts them. For example, a child who expresses great anger when served food which they mildly dislike may do so not because of the temporary displeasure caused by the food but because they are experiencing great inner distress resulting from some unrelated condition. This signal is one to which parents have responded probably immemorially in their practical behavior: when, for example, a young child becomes "difficult" late in the day their behavior is often interpreted (most usually accurately) as reflecting they being "overtired."

2. The second signal is any "puzzling" kind of statement.

    This is a statement which a parent is unable to understand although they sense that the child intends the statement to be communicative. One afternoon I was the guest for cake and coffee of a single parent and her four-year-old daughter. As my "contribution" I had brought a box of small chocolate covered cakes filled with jelly. While her mother made the coffee I sat with the child at the dining room table with a plate of these cakes in front of us. The child took one of the cakes, ate off the chocolate covering, and placed the remainder of the cake on her plate. She then made a brief statement. I no longer recall her words but I do remember that I was completely unable to understand their meaning. I felt a sense of momentary unease about the child, thinking, later, that if her statement to me reflected her usual speech, then she was suffering unhappiness so significant that it was interfering with her ability to communicate with others.

3. The third signal is the failure to respond in an expected manner.

As parents come to "know" a child over an extended period of time they develop expectations about how that child will react when they encounter a particular situation. Thus, if a child typically "throws a tantrum" when faced with frustration, its absence in that circumstance may indicate that the child is experiencing such great distress that they fear they would lose total control and would possibly harm another were they to allow themselves to express their feelings. Likewise, a child who typically grants only perfunctory attention to strangers visiting their home might, were they to greet them effusively and spend considerable time with them, be feeling uncomfortable about some aspect of their life.

4. The fourth signal is less mature behavior than would be expected of a child of a particular chronological age.

Eight year old Albert was brought to my office because of his "hyperactivity." He was (reportedly) continually in motion even in the very small, special, private school class in which he had been placed. While I spoke with his mother, Albert played with one of the toys I keep in a bag in my office. Because the toy he chose (a gun shooting Ping-Pong balls) made a good deal of noise, I asked Albert—after explaining my reasons—to play in the waiting room while I spoke with his mother. He left but returned several minutes later, apparently unable to tolerate being alone. I soon learned the reason why.

When his mother had left the room, Albert told me of the fears which enveloped his life: a monster lay in wait for him in dark corners and terrifying dreams caused him to fear sleep. He had been unable to remain alone in my waiting room because of his overwhelming fear that the monster was there with him. Albert's inability to remain alone, a characteristic usually found only in very young children (or in older children when they are troubled), thus signified that he was experiencing considerable distress.

5. The fifth signal is behavior more mature than would be expected of a child of a particular age.

I don't believe that I'll ever forget Kathy, a small, dark- haired, very bright 4 1/2-year-old girl. She was brought to the clinic by her mother on the advice of her mother's psychotherapist who believed that Kathy might be experiencing psychological difficulties. Because psychological tests can provide a great deal of accurate information very quickly, it was decided to use this method of evaluating Kathy, and I (as the clinical psychologist) was chosen to perform the evaluation. I decided to use a full battery of tests measuring intellectual, personality, and visual-motor aspects of functioning.

As we began the test, Kathy sat at the end of a rectangular table while I sat facing her. After performing several tasks during the intelligence test evaluation, Kathy suddenly left her chair, walked over to my side, and leaned against me. With her shoulder touching mine, Kathy began fingering the buttons on her dress. Soon a button opened and then another as she remarked to me in a matter-of-fact tone of voice, "Oh, the button opened up." The seduction scene performed by this very precocious child could scarcely be improved upon by an adult.

Kathy's surprisingly mature behavior reflected the serious psychological stress she was experiencing, discomfort which was causing her to attempt to flee the pain which pervaded her life as a child by adopting the behavior of an adult.

6. The sixth signal is a sudden, intense fear.

All children (and adults) have fears which trouble them. These fears rarely become visible to others so long as the emotional stress which they represent remains at such a level that it can be tolerated. However, when distress becomes intolerable, irrational fears may surface and become visible. Thus a child who previously never feared sleeping without a night light might now refuse to sleep in a completely dark room.

7. The seventh signal is an intense need for "sameness."

A child, compared to an adult, is a most inadequate person. The child is incapable of obtaining for themselves what they need to survive. They are also incapable of coping with rapid major changes in their environment. In order to feel secure a child attempts to construct a certain order in their life. This need for predictability in one's life is not limited to children. Obviously adults share such a need (as is exemplified by the resistance of most people to making frequent changes in their residence). What is significant is not a need for some moderate measure of predictability, but the intensification of the degree of "sameness" demanded. Thus it would be "normal" for a child to object to such a major change in their life as a new school, but atypical (and thus possibly indicative of considerable distress) were they to become intensely upset if the dinner hour were changed a half hour, or if their preferred pajamas were not available.

8. The eighth signal is behavior which is hyperactive.

There is no one "normal" level of activity. Children have differing personalities: the personality of individual children may "normally" vary from relatively inactive and lethargic to very active and continually seeking new experiences. This signal for concern, reflective of inner distress, occurs when the activity which seems to consume the child reflects not their response to a novel stimulus (like a new toy) or situation (a new experience, the view from atop a building, or the like) but is rather an activity which seems aimless. It then reflects not curiosity but the child's inability to involve themselves in anything. Thus this behavior indicates not pleasure but intense distress. For example, eight-year-old Albert's hyperactivity reflected the intense discomfort which he was experiencing; his external behavior reflected the internal chaos which had enveloped his mind.

9. The ninth signal is behavior which is insufficiently active.

An adult patient of mine, the mother of a teenage boy, telephoned me one summer because her son, Harold, while previously a "normally" active boy, now stayed in bed. Harold spoke to her and ate his meals but had, largely, remained in bed in his room for what was now six days. Some months before she had consulted me about what she considered to be her son's unhappiness. I then spoke with him several times in my office but was unable to involve him in continuing treatment. I now told Harold's mother that I felt he was trying to resolve his unhappiness by nurturing himself: through rest and food and quiet he was attempting to heal himself, to "come together." I advised her not to attempt to change his present behavior. Several days later she reported that Harold had left his bed and was again active and seeing his friends.

Children who sleep for long periods of time or who spend much time "resting" may be attempting to cope with their unhappiness by reducing their involvement with the external environment. The reason for this is that their distress reduces their ability to deal with the additional demands which would be presented through interaction with their friends, their family, their schoolwork, and so on.

These nine Signals for Concern are ways through which a child indicates to us that they are encountering a situation in their environment or an inner conflict with which it is beyond their capacity to cope alone. These signals thus occur naturally throughout childhood and adolescence at periods when our society demands that particular tasks be learned or specific duties performed.

Some of these signals (for example, the need for excessive "sameness") may be evident even in the lives of adults at particular periods of stress. In the next chapter those periods of childhood and adolescence during which a child would naturally be expected to experience difficulty are described. My purpose is to relieve the concern which parents develop at these times. Those situations which demand parents' intervention will be distinguished from situations in which such intervention is best avoided and the child left free to resolve their problem alone, as effectively as they can. And through our scientific examination of these situations we will come to understand the nature of child development, how a child's innate potential interacts with naturally encountered environmental situations to produce a psychologically healthy adult.

Notes

1. K. Bridges, "Emotional Development in Early Infancy," *Child Development* 3 (1932): 324-341.
2. B. Inhelder and J. Piaget, *The Growth of Logical Thinking from Childhood to Adolescence* (New York: Basic Books, 1958).

CHAPTER TWO

When Your Child Must Be Unhappy:
The Periods of Natural Childhood Stress

My experience with children has taught me that while difficulties may arise at any point in a child's development, some periods naturally contain more stress than others. This stress does not derive from the particular personality of the child or their parents, or from the size of their income; nor does it reflect their degree of formal education. It arises from the major demands made upon a child at particular periods of their life when it is required that they learn certain tasks and acquire certain skills. Because the responsibility for instruction in these areas is (sometimes undeservedly) placed upon or accepted by their parents, they too experience this stress.

A child who has lacked certain basic experiences early in their life will have great difficulty meeting these demands when they arise. Because severely disturbed children have often lacked those basic healthy experiences which foster human development, from a study of their lives we can gain important knowledge about the nature of the experiences required by normal children for their healthy emotional and intellectual development.

While treating Robert, an autistic boy, I acquired the most illustrative example in my clinical career of the effect that the lack of certain fundamental experiences early in a child's life can have upon their development.

Robert was the youngest of four boys in a family living in the southern part of the United States. His father was an executive of a large corporation; his mother was a scientist. At our first meeting, Robert's ready smile and courteous and gentle manner served to disguise the enormous suffering which he had endured in his life.

Robert was described by his parents as being an "ideal child" during his infancy; they would have wanted no other. It was several more years before problems were recognized. Robert's difficulties in relating to his parents and to other children then seemed so serious that professional advice was sought. After exhaustive study, several eminent psychiatrists diagnosed Robert as being "autistic"; one described him as "incurable."

When I saw Robert ten years later his difficulties were obvious. He barely related to his external environment and spoke only of clocks, watches, and electric motors. The contrast between Robert's behavior and what I sensed to be his significantly greater intellectual and emotional potential caused me to make that professional commitment to his healing which a psychologist is able to make (because of his limited time) to just one patient at a time: I vowed to myself that I would give Robert whatever he required of my professional attention in order for him to become healed. I vowed that the demands of his life would have priority over my other professional activities and even, if need be, over the demands of my personal life.

During the early months of Robert's psychotherapy he tried to determine whether I was a person worthy of his trust by asking me the same questions on several occasions, weeks and months apart, and comparing my answers. Had I ever traveled across the James River Bridge? Had I ever visited Shenandoah National Park? Had I ever traveled on the Metroliner to Washington? On those occasions when fatigue or a lapse in memory caused me to respond differently from the way I had on another occasion Robert would become silent and look away from me. Several moments would pass before he stated in a surprisingly mature (and somewhat hurt) tone of voice, "But last time you said ..." It would take days for the sudden chill that enveloped our relationship to dissipate.

As time passed I became more comfortable in Robert's presence. My increased liking and compassion for him made more tolerable the stress which his very difficult behavior caused me to feel. This stress did not result from verbal abuse or threats of physical harm. He never called me "ugly," "stupid," "inadequate," "smelly," or "crazy" as had other of my disturbed hospitalized patients. He never spit or broke eggs on my office door or broke my office window. Nor did he thrust a lighted cigarette to within one inch of my eye, a harrowing experience which I endured one afternoon.

But the demand Robert made upon me—that I enter into his madness— was equally severe. Often after he left my office I felt as if my brain were being torn in two, as if I were indeed going mad. At these times I wandered through the corridors of this setting which I term The Hospital, seeking another staff member, any co-worker ranging in position from porter to hospital director, to speak with, to relax the stress I experienced from treating this very damaged boy. But Robert's demand that I risk the stability of my mind in his treatment was no more than he demanded of himself: several months after my first meeting with Robert he risked his life!

It was on a sunny fall day that I first learned of Robert's suicide attempt. Nonchalantly leaving The Hospital, he had walked several miles to a nearby textile factory, climbed over the fence, and touched an exposed high-voltage power line. He escaped harm only because the power had been turned off during factory renovations. He was then noticed by a plant guard who, after a brief conversation, telephoned The Hospital. A car was immediately sent to pick him up.

I'm not proud to admit that my initial emotions upon hearing of Robert's suicide attempt related solely to my self-interest. I felt furious with him: Didn't he realize how his death would have affected me? My professional involvement with him was so great that had he died I could not have conceived of continuing my work as a psychologist. After several minutes of berating Robert to myself my anxiety diminished and I again became able to help him. I went to Robert's room and my statement to him then was very different from those which I had fantasized. I said, "I heard what happened at the factory. You must have been very unhappy to try to kill yourself."

Robert, despite his extremely guarded nature, then described the incident to me. He said that he had begun to think of killing himself that weekend. After he entered the factory he noticed a water fountain with cups alongside. Before touching the power line he drank a cup of water, repeating to himself that this would be the last water he would ever drink, his "last cup of water."*

It was only after the personal crisis that the suicide attempt created for Robert, that crisis which finally forced him to experience fully the depression and anxiety which he had been shielding himself from for much of his life, that our relationship changed. He now became even more dependent upon his contact with me. He spent long periods sitting (or lying) on the bench outside my office waiting for one of his two daily psychotherapy sessions. It was then that we began to play "our games."

---

* This act, reminiscent of Christ's last supper, had a heavily symbolic significance for Robert. Although of Jewish parentage, he had, early in his life, professed a commitment to Christian (particularly Fundamentalist Protestant) theology. As a child he had been a persistent visitor to the Baptist church near his home, often wandering through it for many hours.

While seated in my office one afternoon, Robert spoke of an uncomfortable incident which had occurred in a department store in his hometown. His next words were, "You be the department store man and I'll be Robert. Hello, Mr. Department Store Man." With my response of "Hello, Robert" a new phase of his treatment began. For the next several years this "game," our re-enactment—with changes —of significant events in Robert's past, comprised the major tool of his treatment.

These changes, acting assertive or affirming the desirability of human intimacy, portrayed behavior different from that which occurred during the actual events. Thus Robert used these "games" to experiment, in the security of my company, with greatly feared but healthy attitudes and feelings.

One "game" which seemed of particular significance to him and which we repeated innumerable times, went as follows: I portrayed Karen, a six-year-old girl with whom Robert had been friendly when they both attended a private school for disturbed children. I ("Karen") pretended to hold Robert in my arms and rock him. Repeatedly he stated that being rocked "feels good" and asked whether I enjoyed rocking him. I assured him that I did. Our roles then reversed: I pretended to be Robert and he pretended to be Karen with the same questions and answers being repeated. Through this activity Robert was attempting to provide himself with the nurturing he had never fully experienced as a child.

If I ever question the importance of such basic experiences to the healthy development of a child's intellectual and personality structures, the memory of my experience with Robert will rapidly dissuade me. It was not chance which caused him to want to re-create that nurturing experience appropriate to an infant for he sensed with the penetrating vision often possessed by disturbed children (and adults) its crucial importance in the earliest phase of life.

Because a child is so helpless during their earliest years of life—dependent upon their parents for all that is necessary to sustain life—their capacity for autonomy is very limited. The struggle between a child's innate desire to be autonomous and their inability (because of their intellectual, personality, and physical limitations) to do so has two important consequences:

1. A child is forced to develop mature intellectual capacities (this will be discussed further in Chapter 3).

2. A crucial importance is placed upon they being provided with an adequate parenting experience throughout their earliest years. If a child is provided this experience they will be able to cope more successfully with the natural developmental stresses which they will inevitably encounter. If a child lacks this experience they will be far more likely to encounter significant difficulties throughout their later years.

But it is inaccurate to associate the nurturing or care-taking experience required for a child's healthy development with their mother alone. While the vast majority of such experiences in American society are provided by the biological mother, the essential elements of this experience can be provided by any appropriately responsive, biologically unrelated person of either sex.

What elements of the care-taking experience are crucial in the life of a child?

Essential Elements of a Caretaker ("Mothering") Experience

1. *Attention.* Over the course of our life few words are as hammered into our consciousness as *attention.* This word has come to be used in American society almost as an adjective of praise: it is not unusual to hear a child or adult described as a "good, attentive boy" (or girl, or worker). What seems to be implied is that the person is quiet, predictable, and obedient and that their behavior presents no cause for concern. Are these personality characteristics —quiet, predictable, obedient, unalarming—descriptive of the adequate mother?*

While some characteristics would surely apply (current research suggests that one of the most damaging elements to a child's development is inconsistency in their parents' response to them), few would be favorably impressed by a parent (or a friend) whose predominant personality attributes were these. But the original non-idiomatic meaning of the word attentive—to be observant— is essential to the mothering role.

*For the sake of verbal simplicity, the word "mother" when used throughout this book (unless otherwise indicated, or when a vignette is presented) should be considered to refer to the caretaker parent, who may be of either sex. Similarly, my generalizations about the behavior of children and the responses of parents are accurate and intended for both boys and girls or mothers and fathers regardless of the gender of the pronoun used in the statement.

There are several attributes of attention. One refers to its conscious and focused characteristic: an example is the attentive listening and viewing granted by a student to a teacher who is discussing a forthcoming examination.

Another reflects its associative aspect: combining what one is hearing (or viewing) with previously gained knowledge; an example is a technician listening to a consultant describe a new technical procedure.

A third characteristic is what was described by Freud as "evenly-hovering."[1] Here the person listens or views without consciously attempting to select out any one element but rather allowing his "unconscious memory ... to be given full play.... One has simply to listen and not to trouble to keep in mind anything in particular."[2] This aspect of attention is prominent at times in the practice of psychotherapy. One winter the mother of a boy I was treating died suddenly. Several months before her death he had planned a vacation in Montreal with a group of students from his school. The date of the vacation turned out to be one week after his mother's funeral.

A few days before the departure of the student group he asked my advice: Should he now continue with his planned vacation? I suggested that he do so, adding that it was important, when faced with the death of a valued person, to find some way of affirming a commitment to one's own life. At his next therapy session (after his return from Montreal) he spoke of having suddenly begun crying one afternoon as he was seated alone in his hotel room. My immediate association, deriving from my evenly-hovering attention, was that he was crying over the loss of his mother. But, thinking of his emotionally barren childhood, I rejected this association, saying instead, "You were crying for the loving childhood experience you never had." His response was, "I was crying for my mother." In this instance my temporary distrust of that thought which arose from my evenly-hovering attention had led me to make an unhelpful response.

The attentive attitude of an adequate parent contains all three of these elements (though not simultaneously): it is conscious and focused (toward the child); it is associative (with knowledge of the child's previous usual mode of functioning); and it is evenly-hovering (allowing the parent to relate their personal associations to what they are seeing and hearing of the child's behavior).

2. *Intervention.* Some years ago I was consulted by a highly gifted woman who was in a very anxious state. Possessing both great intelligence and considerable creativity, she was advancing rapidly in her chosen profession. However, her personal life was very difficult. She was tormented, being unable to decide whether to remain with her husband (who provided her with intellectual and emotional companionship but for whom she felt little passion) or choose her lover (toward whom she felt passion but with whom she experienced little intellectual or emotional comradeship).

Despite her repeated demands, I refused to advise her on a course of action. My position throughout her years of treatment (as she drifted from one lover to another) remained the same. I insisted that her dilemma had very complex roots. I added that as she gained greater awareness of what she was experiencing, of her thoughts and feelings, she would gradually make that decision which would be wisest for her. Over the course of her psychotherapy her mention of "the dilemma" gradually became less frequent: rather, she spoke of her childhood experiences with her parents. We often discussed the limited emotional nurturing she had received in her early years. One day she remarked, "Maybe I was spoiled. I always got everything I wanted." I responded, "A spoiled child is one who has everything they want but very little of what they really need."

It is not easy to decide how to intervene most helpfully with a child. Does one instantly satisfy each of their demands (as for food, physical contact, play) or not?

In the mid-1800s an extremely rigid method of child rearing spread from Germany throughout Europe. This method was devised by Dr. Daniel Schreber, a noted physician and orthopedic specialist, a clinical instructor in the medical school of the University of Leipzig and medical director of that city's Orthopedic Institute.[3] This method prescribed the use of various mechanical bodily restraints (resembling medieval torture instruments) to keep a child's posture erect, and the creation of a schedule which would rigidly control each moment of their day: any disobedience was to be punished by the withholding of a meal or by corporal punishment.

The "approved" child care method has changed with each generation. It is fortunate that one need endure only a limited period of existence as a child or parent so discordant and quickly changing are these "approved" methods.

In the American society of the 1920s the feeding of infants at regular intervals was recommended. This method was believed to instill regular habits and "discipline" in the child (a la Dr. Schreber). The child's crying from hunger or other discomfort was to be ignored. Twenty-five years later feeding and emotional nurturing on demand were prescribed.

Using the criteria of popularity, a parent might easily be considered cruel for engaging in unfashionable but formerly acceptable child-rearing techniques. Indeed, over the course of a single generation, what was formerly considered the child-rearing practice of a thoughtful, concerned parent might even come to be considered the sadistic acting out of an unhappy spouse.

In determining how best to intervene with a child when they are troubled, consideration must be given to the child's desire for intervention, to their stage of development, and to the personality of each of their parents.

One must also consider that intervention is not limited to doing something: not to act (or speak) is also a method of intervention and may be the course of action that is most helpful in certain circumstances. Other considerations to be explored before intervening at various periods in a child's development will be presented later in this chapter and in Chapter 5.

3. *Care.* One derivation of the word *care* is the Middle English word *car*, meaning "anxiety"; another is the Old High German word *chara*, meaning *lament*. Thus people sensed long before modern psychology that pain and sorrow are inevitably associated with the taking of responsibility for another's life. Occasionally I've had to speak to a patient in ways and of matters which I knew would hurt them deeply; but they had to hear these words and to experience this pain if they were to grow.

Thus I once said to a patient, "Who do you think you are? Your daddy's beautiful girl? You think the world will support you once you leave this hospital? You have very serious conflicts and if you don't solve them you'll likely die at an early age in a welfare hotel." The girl began crying, tears running down her cheeks. She said, "Dr. Goldstein, you hurt me." I knew that what I said had hurt her deeply. It hurt me to speak this way to her. Yet was it not more caring for me to cause her to experience temporary pain than to allow her future years to become even more tormented than her past had been?

Similarly a parent must occasionally speak and act in ways which cause a child temporary pain but which make more probable their future healthy development. To allow a child's probable reaction to determine their parents' behavior is to reverse the roles of parent and child, causing damage to the lives of both.

4. *Faith.* Being a helpful parent requires one to have faith that a child who is provided appropriate nurturing

will develop into a healthy adult. This faith or confidence in the future must underlie all of the care-taking activities provided for the child. This optimism about the course of a child's life does not derive from ignorance or agreement with the latest "pop" psychology magazine article but reflects a knowledge of the fundamental elements of human development and change. My clinical experience over the years has strengthened my belief in the old adage which states that it is the doctor's treatment which heals but nature which grants the cure.

Emotional nurturing, intellectual stimulation, and physical care enable a child to grow, but their genetic heritage sets the limits and provides the broad pathways within which their development occurs. And as nature guides the child into seeking those experiences which (granted the best of fortune) will enable them to optimize their growth and (with poorer fortune) will promote their healing, so too are their parents guided by their own natures into providing them with or seeking for them those experiences which they require, though they may occasionally distrust (and thus ignore) that course of action which their intuition tells them is correct.

To have faith in the future of one's child means to trust in the wisdom of nature, to believe that each physically healthy child, because they are human, has the potential for healthy emotional and intellectual development, and that the vast majority of emotional disturbances, if provided appropriate treatment, can be healed.

I feel very uneasy when the parents of a patient tell me that their child grew up "without problems," for this is not possible. What is probable is that their memory of the difficulties which both they and their child experienced has faded over the years. A psychologist once asked mothers to recall significant medical ("health") events in their child's life. He then compared these memories to the original hospital and clinic records which described the events as they occurred. The psychologist found major differences between the memories and the actual events,**4**

What caused these discrepancies? Many rapid changes occur during particular periods of a child's development. These changes affect the parents as well as the child for both must continually readjust themselves to the child's changing needs. The major (but often unrecognized) stress produced by these rapid changes is the cause of a mother's inability to remember accurately certain events in her child's life. It is fortunate that the feelings of anxiety and depression which these events cause can be forgotten: Who would voluntarily wish to re-experience all the events of one's early years (as either child or parent)?

Little can be done to avoid these stresses completely, for they are intrinsically associated with human development, but an awareness of their nature and of the most effective means of coping with them can do much to reduce a parent's level of anxiety when they occur. Just as the injection of microorganisms may secure immunity to a physical disease, so too can an awareness of the existence and nature of an impending psychological stress provide a "psychological inoculation" which reduces the discomfort caused by that stress.

In a child's life there are four naturally occurring periods of rapid change during which they experience considerable stress and make major demands upon their parents for understanding, comfort, and assistance. These are:

1. The initial months of life when they are being integrated into the family
2. Their early period of training
3. The time when they are making initial attempts to form relationships outside of their family and to acquire basic social and educational skills

4. The period of adolescence when their sexual interests increase, their systematic self-exploration begins, and they attempt to become independent of their family.

The Earliest Period of Life

The beginning is always difficult.
—Arthur Schopenhauer

Even more remarkable than the large number of children who experience difficulty in their earliest years are the relatively large number of parents who regard the existence of these difficulties as being unusual. The high frequency of divorce in today's society provides evidence of the difficulty of integrating two carefully chosen individuals into one family unit. Why then should we not expect the integration of an unselected infant into the ongoing lives of two people to provide a stressful experience for all concerned?

Many of the children I treat would not have remained in their family setting at all if the divorce of a child from their family existed as a viable alternative. I have yet to meet an eight-year-old child who has successfully packed his suitcase and moved out of their house but I have met many children of that age and younger who have tried it.

The major difficulty experienced by the child during their first several years derives from the necessity to "mesh" their unique personality with the personalities of their parents.*

*A study by James Cameron, Ph.D., "Parental Treatment, Children's Temperament, and the Risk of Childhood Behavioral Problems: Initial Temperament, Parental Attitudes, and the Incidence and Form of Behavioral Problems," reported in the January 1978 issue of *The American Journal of Orthopsychiatry*, provided evidence of this.

Each child's behavior reflects their particular combination of personality characteristics. Some children are naturally easy to get along with: their behavior is regular and predictable, and they respond positively and adapt themselves readily to new situations. Other children's temperaments would be difficult for most parents to cope with: they tend to withdraw from new situations and to adapt slowly; often they are easily distracted.

Whether a child has a temperament that is "easy" or "difficult" for their parents to interact with is not determined by the nature of that temperament but by the stress which it creates for the child and their parents. This stress is determined by the difference between those behavioral characteristics which the parents consider desirable and those exhibited by their child. Thus what is significant is not the particular personality of a child or the particular personality of each of their parents but the degree to which these personalities can interact satisfactorily.

Because each individual is unique there is no way to avoid some stress whenever any two or more people interact: the only meaningful goal is to attempt to reduce this discomfort to a tolerable level.

SURVIVING AS A PARENT THROUGHOUT YOUR CHILD'S INFANCY: DO'S AND DON'TS

Do Study Your Infant!
One of the behavioral characteristics which parents find most difficult to tolerate is the child's particular level of activity or excitability. They may be considered either too active or not active enough. This characteristic is an important one, for two major studies of normal children

have found an infant's characteristic level of activity to persist from birth through adolescence and perhaps beyond.5,6 Several other characteristics also have a strong biological basis and are therefore highly resistant to change: the degree to which an infant responds to sounds and sights; the degree to which they nurture themselves (as by thumb sucking and stroking their skin); their tendency to play alone spontaneously; the way they respond when they are uncomfortable (hungry or tired); and their pattern of response to physical objects and people.

Do Question Your Values!
No particular manner of behavior is inherently more or less useful in adapting to life though some may seem to be. Life in today's society has caused us to believe that there is but one kind of child with the necessary attributes for success: their mood is continually positive; their reactions are regular, predictable, and mild; and they are readily adaptable and tend to respond with interest to new situations.

While possessing these characteristics may be an asset in some vocations or educational experiences, few leading figures in any area of American society could be so described. For example, many of those industrialists who have been considered outstanding in the restoration of financially troubled companies exhibited latent paranoid personality characteristics and very difficult behavior.7

No temperamental characteristic is inherently "bad" or "maladaptive." For example, a child who is easily distracted may have a greater capacity, than one who is less easily distracted, for responding to continually changing situations.

Do Accept Your Child's Temperament!
Unless actual physical or psychological difficulties are present, your child's temperament reflects their basic biological structure. Any attempt to alter their behavior

permanently will be futile and uncomfortable for the both parents and their child. But no older child, regardless of temperament, has the right to be continually discourteous or to refuse to perform family chores. Temperament refers to the manner of and not the capacity for performance.

Don't Feel Guilty For Making "Mistakes"!

A "mistake" occurs when a parent relates to a child in such a manner as to cause them excessive discomfort (for example, yelling loudly at an infant), or in some other way fails to respond to their needs in a manner that is most nurturing of their emotional and intellectual development. But these mistakes are inevitable. The infant and their parents are strangers to one another. It takes time for each to learn the needs and capacities of the other. After this occurs, fewer mistakes will happen. What is important to an infant's development is not that there be no mistakes but that the child feels continually cared for. An infant will "forgive" errors if he feels that these are unintentional. But he will not forgive disinterest.

Don't Feel That You Must Devote Your Life To Your Infant!

An infant acquires knowledge by constructing their own theories of the nature of people and of objects. (This will be discussed further in Chapter 3.) To do this, they use the data at hand: the behavior of their parents and others who interact with them and those objects which surround them (their toys, bottle, playpen, and so forth). Although contact with others is certainly necessary for healthy development, an infant's learning occurs even when they are alone. Their development is fostered even when they are asleep!

A newborn infant experiences that state of sleep described as rapid eye movement (REM) sleep for one-third of their total early existence. It is believed that during these periods of sleep much internal arousal of the brain is occurring. This fosters the development of the infant's mind and helps to compensate for the relatively minimal external stimulation present during their early life.[8]

Your Child's Early "Training"

A child must acquire certain behavior in their early years in order to function successfully in American society. These "manners" are not very different from those in most other cultures. They comprise the child's mastery of their society's approved methods for the expression and satisfaction of their physiological needs. The importance that American society places upon a child's being trained in these approved methods can be understood when one considers the shame which even adults may feel when they unintentionally violate the norms.

A psychologist in his fifties told me the following story. He had been on a strict high-protein diet for a week and celebrated its termination by eating a piece of heavily frosted chocolate layer cake. Several hours later he went fishing in a stream some distance from his house. Because of the rain and his activity he was heavily dressed in rubber waders and protective clothing. Suddenly he felt an intense urge to have a bowel movement. Realizing that he could not reach home quickly enough, he attempted to loosen his heavily layered and buttoned fishing gear. Unable to do so, he then experienced that "accident" which parents most decry. He reported that the intense feelings of embarrassment and humiliation he experienced provided him with a vivid insight into the childhood experiences described by his adult patients.

Those physiological needs with which our society is most concerned comprise feeding, elimination, and sexual expression. But there are vast differences in the effects that training in each of these areas has on a child. While weaning frees a child from reliance on their mother and thereby increases their capacity for independent action, their acquiring the "approved" method of elimination provides them with little more than discomfort—or perhaps less discomfort than experiencing their parents' anger were they not to behave "properly." Fear alone, if sufficiently intense, can force virtually any child to behave in accordance with their parents' wishes, but only at significant cost to their emotional and intellectual development.

Raymond was a nine-year-old boy living in a large metropolitan area. He was a severe bed wetter. On only rare mornings were his bed sheets dry. Finally, his mother could no longer contain her fury at her inability to change his behavior. Dragging him by the arm into the kitchen, she grabbed a large knife and, after thrusting it in front of him she said, "If you wet your bed one more night I'm going to cut off your padderwacky!" Raymond never wet his bed again. By tying a large rubber band tightly around his penis before he went to sleep, Raymond avoided having to test his mother's resolve.

While the experience of emotional stress and the use of implicit threats are unavoidable if a child is to acquire the socially desired physiological "skills," a parent with the proper perspective will attain the "success without damage" they seek.

SURVIVING YOUR CHILD'S EARLY TRAINING or DOES IT EVER END? DO'S AND DON'TS

Do Relax!

Virtually all children eventually become toilet trained. But this does take time. A research report based upon the study of 859 children (male and female, African-American and white) for twelve years stated that by age six 96 percent of the children were consistently "dry" during the day, while 77 percent were consistently "dry" during the night. Yet at age nine 10 percent of the girls still had periodic nighttime "accidents," and 10 percent of the boys were not fully trained at age eleven.[9]

Do *Appreciate The Complexity Of The Training!*
A child is not a machine. A change in their behavior in one area has ramifications in others. When it is demanded of a child that they change their manner of elimination, their sense of autonomy is being infringed upon. When they are instructed not to handle their genitals in public, they are also acquiring the idea that one part of their body is, for some reason, "special." A change in their eating habits from feeding by their mother to eating autonomously also significantly reduces the amount of interaction they have with another person.

Don't *allow yourself to become over*-involved in any one area of your child's development!
A child's cognitive skills, social knowledge, and physiological abilities develop simultaneously. The child is always more than just a bed wetter or a poor eater. Your excessive concern with any one area of their life will reduce their own degree of interest in other (perhaps more important) areas of their development. For example, it is far more significant to a child's future that they gain a sense of confidence about their ability to interact effectively with others than that they be toilet trained by 3½ years.

Don't *Set Rigid Goals!*
There have been only a very few times in my clinical experience when a mother's description of her child's behavior caused me to burst out laughing. Karen was a very pretty four-year-old girl. Her mother, exasperated over her repeated bed-wetting, demanded that this cease! Karen was severely spanked after each nighttime "accident." Her bed-wetting immediately ceased. No longer did Karen awake each morning with a wet bed sheet. Now each night she left her bed and urinated on the floor.

The social pressures which an untrained child experiences are very great. No child would willingly accept the embarrassment and humiliation which their inability to control their basic physiological mechanisms presents to themselves. If a child persists in behavior which their parents and others find uncomfortable (soiling themselves, continually touching their genitals, and the like), it is because they have little choice in the matter. To criticize a child for that over which they have little control is cruel and will lower their already inadequate self-esteem. And to set rigid goals is to presume that both child and parents have total understanding of what are usually very complicated situations.

Early Peer and School Experiences

The stress associated both with a child's earliest friendships and with their initial school experiences derive from a similar cause: both represent the first contacts they have outside of their immediate family. The poet Robert Frost once remarked that only your family will never refuse to admit you when you come to visit. Similarly, a child is granted unconditional acceptance only by their parents (to the best of their ability) and risks rejection and failure once they leave their family setting.

While few would deny that the occasional cruelty of young children and the frequent inadequacies of many school settings add unnecessary difficulties to this period of childhood, it is also undeniable that most children emerge from this period having achieved only varying degrees of success. Why? How can parents increase the probability that their child will succeed in the tasks they face at this time in their life?

HELPING YOUR CHILD THROUGH THEIR EARLY PEER AND SCHOOL EXPERIENCES OR WHEN YOUR CHILD LOOSENS THEIR TIES, MUST YOU LOSE YOUR MIND? DO'S AND DON'TS

Do *Rejoice*!

You're regaining your freedom. Your child's growing independence from their family frees you from the necessity of having continually to minister to their needs. How do you plan to use your extra time to add more enjoyment to your life?

Do *expect your child to feel hurt!*

When your child moves out into the world, meeting children their own age and entering school, they will begin to test their abilities against those of their peers. They will also begin attempting to meet those expectations which society in general, as interpreted through the eyes of their schoolteacher and other adults outside the family, demand of them. It is inevitable and also desirable that some of their experiences end in failure: from these they will gain an accurate assessment of their abilities. It is also inevitable that you will feel wounded when your child is hurt physically (when they are hit by another child) or emotionally. Almost certainly too your wound will require more time to heal than your child's.

Don't *Expect Your Child To Share Your Limitations!*

I once treated, in a hospital setting, a severely disturbed seven-year-old boy, Billy. Many emotionally disturbed children appear no different from healthy children. Billy did. Thin and wiry, with a sallow complexion, his anxiety caused him to be continually in motion. Because of his desire to be free of the hospital confines, we began having therapy sessions outdoors, on the very beautiful hospital grounds, instead of in my office. My readiness to agree to his suggestion that we move outdoors was also influenced by the state of my office after a 45-minute session with him: when his angry feelings exceeded his very limited capacity to contain them, he would upset the large cardboard box holding the playing cards, stuffed animals, crayons, paints, and other toys used by my child patients during their therapy sessions, and fling these objects about the room.

It was on a lovely spring day when we began our outdoor sessions. But ten seconds after we left my office Billy ran from my side. He dashed out the building exit and vanished from sight. My anxiety increased when I saw him some minutes later, high in the branches of a tree. For the next few therapy sessions I was more concerned with his physical elevation than his psychological distress.

Billy's climbing had placed him in no personal danger: my subsequent questioning of the attendants revealed that he was a truly extraordinary climber, far and away the best among the children at the hospital. But his behavior made me very anxious. Throughout my youth in New York City I (and probably a not insignificant number of other children) had considered tree climbing to be a highly dangerous and foolhardy, if not an actually illegal action. Thus my reaction to Billy's behavior reflected *my* fear rather than his danger. In a similar manner, parents may attempt to prevent their child from engaging in activities which *they* feared during their childhood. Or they may force the child before they are ready to engage in certain activities (as, swimming) because they are determined that they not grow to maturity fearing them as their parents did.

Adolescence

It would be illogical for an adolescent not to be concerned with sex since the definitive criteria for the attainment of adolescence is that a child has achieved the capacity for reproduction.

Several years ago I was consulted by the teacher of a fifteen-year-old boy who was in treatment with me. She was convinced that he was suffering from a serious learning disability. She described Tim's inability to attend to classwork, his frequent "gazing into the air," and the careless arithmetic and grammatical errors which filled his lessons. Her vehemence caused me to question my long held belief about the cause of Tim's limitations. I knew that he had very serious emotional difficulties and I believed that these affected his ability to perform in school. But I was convinced (because of my own clinical intuition and based upon data from psychological and neurological evaluations) that he suffered from no organically derived learning impairment. Could I and the other clinicians be wrong?

At Tim's next therapy session I described his teacher's concern about his academic difficulties. He was unperturbed. Finally I asked him, "Tim, what do you think about in class?" His response was brief and totally explanatory. "I think about girls," he said.

While the difficulties experienced in each period of natural stress derive partially from unresolved earlier difficulties, this factor is particularly influential in determining whether a child successfully surmounts their adolescence. A child must have acquired basic social, educational, and psychological skills in order for them to realize those distinctive goals of adolescence: achieving the capacity for a satisfying sexual relationship, gaining a secure sense of who they are, and acquiring independence from their parents and teachers. If they are unable to achieve these goals they may develop a pseudo mature facade, one which may appear "real" to the casual observer but which will interfere with their healthy future development.

SURVIVING YOUR CHILD'S ADOLESCENCE or IT DOES END! DO'S AND DON'TS

DO EXPECT YOUR ADOLESCENT TO BEHAVE ERRATICALLY SOMETIMES!

Adolescence is a period during which a child's contradictory tendencies exist simultaneously. For example, their feelings may change very quickly from euphoria to gloom; egotism may be followed by humility. And the lust which is never very far from their mind may sorely conflict with their pure ideals.

Wanting to be independent yet being bound to their parents, fearing to lose their old identity but sensing its inadequacy for coping with new challenges, the adolescent's occasionally erratic behavior reflects their inner turmoil, the upheaval that is necessary for the dissolution of their old identity in preparation for the new.[10,11,12]

DO CONTINUE TO MAKE APPROPRIATE DEMANDS OF YOUR ADOLESCENT!

In contrast with their earlier years (from eight to twelve) the adolescent will tend to resent attempts to impose structure upon their life. The greater their fear of independence, the more marked will be their expression of anger toward the proper restrictions which their parents attempt to impose upon their life. Their opposition to these demands is, at least partially, their defense against their underlying yearning for them.

DON'T EXAGGERATE THE SIGNIFICANCE OF ANY ONE STATEMENT OR BEHAVIOR OF YOUR ADOLESCENT!

A major task of the adolescent is to construct a new, stable identity, a new sense of who they are. During this process they will experiment with different theories and behaviors, and "try on" new but transient personality facades. Few indeed will continue to exist as any major aspect of their ultimate identity.

The Middle Ground in Parent Behavior Between Intervening and "Doing Nothing"

Once, while working in a hospital, I was confronted on a Friday afternoon by the problem of how best to prevent the suicide of a seriously disturbed boy. Gradually during the staff conference that ensued there developed two points of view. Dr. R. believed that the "treatment of choice" would be the prescription of antidepressant medication. I opposed this course of action stating:

1. Antidepressant medication required at least several days to become effective; and
2. Because the boy had been newly admitted to the hospital we did not yet know him well enough to prescribe any radical change in his present program of treatment. I recommended that we wait, alert the nursing staff to the situation, and observe his behavior closely over the following days. If other measures then seemed indicated (prescription of medication, restriction of his freedom) these could be carried out.

At the end of the conference Dr. R. stated, with his usual honesty and bluntness, that he found it "very difficult to consider that an appropriate course of action for a crisis might be to do nothing." I responded that we weren't "doing nothing" for to continually monitor a patient's situation, being ever ready to intervene, was certainly to provide them with something very significant and important. My recommended course of action was followed and, happily, the boy's self-destructive behavior disappeared over the course of the following week.

Dr. R.'s belief is, unfortunately, shared by many parents. If they sense their child to be unhappy they rush to do or to say something, virtually unaware of the impact that inappropriate words or actions might have on a child.

The appropriate question is not whether to intervene for parents are always intervening in their child's life. It was Jean Piaget who emphasized the fact that *thought is action*: to think about an object is also to act upon it though this action is internal (mental). Thus the careful and thoughtful ways in which parents continually view their child's life experiences are indeed interventions, though being passive in nature. When are active interventions appropriate?

It is inevitable that a child will experience a moderate degree of stress in the course of their development. But too much stress can damage a child. When they experiences continual stress which it is beyond their capacity to tolerate, then their behavioral and psychological capacities will begin to deteriorate. If the stress persists, the deterioration of their physical organs will follow.

Parents should intervene actively in their child's life when they first realize that the stress they are experiencing is continual and beyond their capacity to endure. The nine Signals for Concern described in the previous chapter, if they persist for more than several days, represent the child's indication to us that they require intervention which is greater than observation in their life.

If the stress does not reach this level or lasts for only a brief period of time, parents should avoid intervening in their child's life, difficult though this may be: witnessing their child's mild discomfort is often more painful to parents than is the actual discomfort to their child.

Intervention should be avoided in these situations for two reasons:

1. A child's experiencing and overcoming a moderate level of stress enables them to develop ways of coping independently with these experiences: the purpose of childhood is to prepare one for an independent existence.
2. Though uncomfortable, the experience of a moderate degree of stress causes a child to question the adequacy of their conclusions about their life experiences, thus fostering their change when this is necessary.

Those techniques which parents may use to reduce a child's discomfort when active intervention is necessary will be discussed in Chapter 5.

Not all of the difficulties which children experience result from the natural stresses of childhood. Some derive from those differences in psychological capacity between children and adults of which neither is aware. Difficulties in communication then result, occasioning serious stress for both the child and their parents. It is this kind of stress and those techniques which are useful in its reduction with which Chapter 3 is concerned.

1. Sigmund Freud, "Recommendations for Physicians on the Psychoanalytic Method of Treatment" (1912), in *Therapy and Techniques* (New York: Collier Books, 1963), p. 118.

2. Ibid., p. 119.

3. William G. Niederland, *The Schreber Case: Psychoanalytic Profile of a Paranoid Personality* (New York: Quadrangle/New York Times Book Company, 1974).

4. C. Wenar, "The Reliability of Mothers' Histories," *Child Development* 33 (1962): 453-462.

5. J. Kagan and H. A. Moss, *Birth to Maturity: A Study in Psychological Development* (New York: John Wiley, 1962).

6. E. S. Schaefer and N. Bayley, "Maternal Behavior, Child Behavior, and Their Intercorrelations from Infancy through Adolescence." *Monographs of the Society for Research in Child Development*, Vol. 28, no. 3 (1963).

7. M. F. R. Kets De Vries, "Crisis Leadership and the Paranoid Potential: An Organizational Perspective," *Bulletin of the Menninger Clinic,* Vol. 41, no. 4 (July 1977):349-365.

8. H. P. Roffwarg, J. H. Muzio, and W. C. Dement, "Ontogenetic Development of the Human Sleep-Dream Cycle," *Science* 152 (1966): 604-619.

9. W. C. Oppel, P. A. Harper, and R. V. Rider, "The Age of Attaining Bladder Control," *Pediatrics*, Vol. 42, no. 4 (1968): 614-626.

10. E. H. Erikson, *Childhood and Society* (New York: W. W. Norton, 1950).

11. E. Z. Friedenberg, *The Vanishing Adolescent* (Boston: Beacon Press, 1959).

12. R. E. Nixon, "An Approach to the Dynamics of Growth in Adolescence," *Psychiatry,* Vol. 24 (1961): 18-31.

CHAPTER THREE

Of Children's Minds and Parents' Myths

I have often thought that the major difficulty which parents have in rearing their children is that they have forgotten their own experiences as children. Remembering primarily their adult experiences, they nevertheless formulate certain conclusions about the nature of a child's behavior and how best to interact with them.

Some of these conclusions are indeed valid and have been used from time immemorial. One, that depriving a troublesome child of a desired pleasure will alter their future behavior, has even been the basis for a popular but naive theory of human motivation: that most human behavior is caused by the desire for pleasure and the fear of punishment. But many conclusions are not valid.

The manner in which parents derive both their valid and their invalid theories of child behavior are identical: by observing and interpreting their child's behavior from a particular perspective. It is because most parents lack the proper scientific perspective on child development and behavior and not because of the observational technique they use that erroneous conclusions occur. And it is their behavior based on these false conclusions which causes needless stress between parents and young children in the earliest years of their interaction.

The observational technique which parents have intuitively used to try to understand the behavior of their children is precisely that method which created the most momentous theory in the field of child psychology in the twentieth century. It was this theory that Albert Einstein described as being "so simple that only a genius could have thought of it." The genius was Professor Jean Piaget of the University of Geneva (Switzerland). His theory can be accurately (although certainly not completely) described in just one sentence: children think differently than adults.

I once visited a day-care center for young children in a large Midwest city. Privately funded and boasting the most modern facilities, the center might have been a model institution were it not for its severe overcrowding: the rooms seemed wall-to-wall with children.

One little boy (about four years old) sat alone in a corner holding a stuffed animal in his arms. He viewed me silently as I approached him. When I was five feet away from him he yelled, "Stop! Don't come into my house! You'll wake my dog." I apologized for my intrusion and walked away. Were an adult to have spoken in a comparable manner I would have regarded him as mad, for the walls of the house and the vivacity of the animal existed only in the child's mind. But I knew that to that child the house and the animal were real even if only for that moment, and that I had without his permission intruded into his world, and for this I apologized.

Were a child's concept of the world to be totally different from that of their parents there could be no communication between them. It is because there are both differences and similarities in their approach to events that difficulties in communication occur.

Many years ago I compared (as part of a research project) the different concepts which children of various ages (four to five years, eight to nine years, and so on) have of the nature of "a baby," "a person their own age," and "a grown-up person." Johnny, the sturdily built 4½-year-old child of a neighbor, served as a subject in this study. After allowing Johnny time to relax by speaking with him about his toys and his friends, I began to question him. "What is a baby?" "A baby is someone who cries a lot and drinks from a bottle," he said. "What is a person your own age?" "He goes to school and doesn't cry," he responded. "And an adult?" I asked. "An adult is married and drives a car and goes to work." "What am I?" I asked him. "Oh, you're an adult!" he said with certainty. "Do I drink from a bottle?" "Oh, nooooo," was his assured, smiling response. My response to his answer was to pull a baby bottle from a box and begin sucking vigorously on it. "Look, Johnny—I'm sucking on this bottle!" He shrugged, "No, you're not." "No, Johnny, I am!" I insisted, now energetically sucking even more noisily on the bottle. Johnny looked at me with amazement and yelled excitedly, "Oh, if you were weally sucking on a bottle I'd wun away." For several days thereafter Johnny gave me a wary look when I passed him on the street.*

What was there about Johnny's thinking which was so different from that of an adult? Surely it was not his associating people of various ages with particular characteristics. What was significant was his unwavering belief in the unessential characteristics he chose or, using more technical language, his self-centeredness (*egocentrism*) and his *concreteness*.

*This incident occurred during my earliest days as a graduate student and I still feel uncomfortable about it. While I have no fear that Johnny was harmed by his participation in the study, I'm not at all sure that the consequences experienced by any very young child who is involved in research where deception is used as a technique can be totally eliminated through their later discussion with the psychologist performing the study. In recent years there has been much criticism (by psychologists) of the use of deception in psychological research on both ethical and scientific grounds.

The Self-Centered Nature
of a Child's Thought

The self-centeredness of a child derives from the gross inadequacies with which they are forced to confront the world in their early years. Unable to provide themselves with even the most necessary elements of physical survival (food, clothing, shelter) a child is totally dependent upon the concern of their parents. If we were (magically) to confront the world as a newborn infant, what would we experience?

The clarity of our vision would be poor, so poor that we would be unable to see the big E were we able to take a standard adult eye examination,[1] and we would be unable to recognize familiar objects such as a bottle.[2] We could perform independently only those activities which were relatively (biologically) autonomous (eating, elimination, breathing). And even some of these functions would require parental aid. It is through the infant's need to be cared for by others that they soon gains a sense of the existence of a world larger than themselves. And from their physical activities (for example, their attempt to grasp a desired object) they gain a rudimentary sense of the boundaries and limitations of their body.

The way that a child relates to the world (after their initial months of life) is not by random hit-or-miss activity, but by constructing a theory of their world which governs their behavior, a theory encompassing all that is important to their existence. And when over the course of time the theory becomes inadequate, no longer enabling them to manipulate effectively the events in their life (which has now become more complex), the theory will be changed to a more adequate one. But as many elements of the former theory as possible will be retained in the new theory.

The development of an infant's mental theory of their environment may be understood by recalling how they physically pick up an unfamiliar object. First they try to pick it up as they did other objects in their past experience. If this is unsuccessful they try a new method, using those techniques from their previous experience in "picking up objects" which are useful. Thus the infant changes the way they relate to the new object, some of their behavior now being "old" and some "new."

Similarly an adult learning to drive an automobile with a standard shift mechanism will find useful the skills (use of the brake, the technique of steering, and the like) formerly gained when they learned to operate an automobile with an automatic transmission. But both the infant and the adult (of these illustrations) will be unable to use their previously learned skills (and to pick up the object or to drive the automobile) if the object or automobile is very different from any which they have previously manipulated.

When a child is confronted by a new experience, they will try to fit this experience into their previously constructed "theory" of the environment. Thus a child soon discovers from their play activity that all objects which are small enough for them to grasp can be moved. Their later activity with, for example, round objects will cause them to amend this "theory" to include the fact that round objects can also be rolled.

But when they are confronted with an event which is totally different from those they have previously encountered, one which does not fit within their already established theories, they will feel distress. As when the familiar routine of their life is suddenly shattered by the absence of their usual care-taking figure or a formerly friendly pet begins to "snap." Experiences which cannot be integrated into previously formed theories of their environment will remain apart from them, existing in their life as permanent objects of distress when they become aroused.

This admittedly simplified description of the development of an infant's intellect is also, nevertheless, relevant to an understanding of the child's emotional development, because a particular kind of emotional disturbance (a neurosis) may be described as consisting of those uncomfortable thoughts and feelings which have remained unintegrated since earliest childhood (this will be discussed further in Chapter 6).

So, as we have seen, a child constructs a theory of their environment using the data of their experience and their immature intellectual abilities. Thus an infant's early experience of being fed each time they are hungry provides evidence for their theory that they are omnipotent—have unlimited power—because it creates their belief that it is their hunger which causes the food to be produced. And it is the immaturity of their intellectual apparatus, their lack of perspective and their inability to analyze their own thinking, which causes them also to consider themselves omniscient, that they possess infinite knowledge.

But the child's sense of omnipotence is shattered early in their life at the time when their feelings of discomfort are not followed—quickly enough—by the comforting attention of their parents. But their theory of omniscience is retained (to a great extent) through adolescence.

Both a child's belief in their omniscience, that they know *everything*, and their self-centeredness create major difficulties in the communication between them and their parents.

Why does a child construct such theories rather than learn all of the possible sequences of events in their life by rote? The motivation for this activity is innate: a human's biological structure compels them to do so. Why the capacity to analyze the environment and to construct a theory of its nature became genetically dominant cannot seriously be questioned considering its value in aiding the survival of the individual.

The "Magic" Present in a Child's Thought

The "magic" present in a child's thought does not refer to their belief in the existence of demons, fairies, or magical incantations (although these may be present). It refers to a type of thinking which is far more extensive in children but not totally absent in adults.

Goethe has written, "In my youthful years when I have been out walking, the sensation of longing for some desired girl has overfallen me, and I thought long enough about it until I really met her."

The belief that one's mind can influence objects and events pervades the thinking of young children. It reflects their lack of awareness of the concept of chance: the knowledge that events which occur contiguous with a thought are not caused by that thought. It also reflects the child's grandiose conception of their own abilities, their belief that they are capable of affecting all events in their environment. This belief in turn reflects the child's continuous desire to understand the nature of their world though their inadequate knowledge of the world sometimes causes them to make glaring errors.

Adults too make such mistakes when they possess erroneous or limited information. Walter was an eight-year- old boy I was seeing for individual psychotherapy. Because he was my last patient of the day, I usually left the clinic soon after the completion of his session. When I got home one Wednesday evening I received a telephone call from the clinic: Walter's mother, contrary to her usual behavior, had not yet picked him up. Since the clinic was about to close, the difficulty was obvious: what should be done with Walter? I telephoned his home and, receiving no answer, drove to the clinic. I again telephoned Walter's mother: silence. With the imminent closing of the clinic there seemed no alternative but to take Walter home with me until his mother could be located. Several minutes after our arrival at my home I managed to locate his mother: she had forgotten that Wednesday was his scheduled afternoon at the clinic and reported his "kidnapping" to the police when he didn't arrive home at the usual time. Thus, forgetting one small piece of information had caused Walter's mother to become involved in an elaborate and dramatic series of events.*

The Role of Truth in a
Child's Speech

A five-year-old patient told me the following story: her ten-year-old cousin had just married and given birth to a baby boy; she and her cousin had recently spent the afternoon caring for the new baby. My response to her story was to exclaim, with a facial expression combining astonishment, surprise, delight, and belief, "Really?" The girl happily and smugly assured me that this was true.

Although the child's statement sounds like delusional thinking, it actually reflected the immaturity of her mind and not psychopathology.

*After this event I always insisted that the parent or guardian of all of the children I treat remain in the waiting room during their child's therapy session. Had this event occurred today in a medical setting, the Department of Social Services would be telephoned to take charge of the child. But this clinic was in a bequeathed building far from the main academic campus and the small staff there was not then so knowledgeable.

Children often make statements more to play with their mental abilities than to describe events accurately. Truth is an adult concept: it is established by comparing one's belief to actual events and rejecting the former if the facts do not support it. The capacity for this type of thinking, involving hypotheses and the establishment of their validity, is fully achieved only at the time of adolescence.

A young child is not fully capable of studying their speech. Thus, if pressed about the truth of an assertion they will—sensing their inadequacy and becoming fearful—even more fervently assert the truth of their statement or become angry and sulk. This response is not peculiar to children: many adults, when pressed about the accuracy of their assertions on a subject about which they have little authoritative information, will respond with vehemence and anger.

Your Child Is Not Brain-Damaged or Why a Child Repeats Their Behavior (Seemingly Interminably)

One of the most important and brilliant statements in the science of child development is Jean Piaget's hypothesis that an infant's instinctual repetition of their earliest reflex reactions leads first to their using these reactions with varying objects and then to their recognition of the differences between each of these objects.

This hypothesis is important not only because it explains a child's repetitive behavior but also because it clarifies how, soon after birth, a child's intellectual abilities begin to evolve!

In layman's language, it means that a newborn child explores their environment through their basic biological activity such as sucking and eating. The child learns the nature of objects by manipulating them during these activities, building up a body of knowledge first about these particular objects and later about similar objects. By repeatedly handling both the same and different objects, a child gradually begins to recognize the nature of various objects and how best to manipulate each one. For example, early in their life a child learns about objects through sucking, first his finger and then other objects (his blanket, rattle, and so on). By sucking different objects, they gain knowledge of their nature. Thus a child's repetitive behavior is essential to their learning about objects and their abilities.

His repetition is little different from the repetitiveness of an adult who is learning a new skill, although the child's need for repetition is greater because of the immaturity of their mind.

Your Child Does Not Possess a Criminal Nature (Although They May Seem To)

I had arrived at a dinner party and met the hostess's four-year-old son. His mother warned him not to touch the bowls of cheese dip and crackers on a table and then left us alone together. Several moments after her departure the boy began sampling the dip with his finger. When I reminded him of his mother's admonition, he responded, "She's not here now."

I cannot believe that there is an adult who has not witnessed a similar event. Such behavior does not, however, indicate an impending massive increase in the crime rate but rather that a child's concept of morality evolves much like their awareness of the nature of truth. Early in their life children define right and wrong in terms of whether or not an action will call forth punishment; only after many years of social, emotional, and intellectual development is a child's behavior determined by the expectations of others and by their sense of guilt for not living up to those expectations.

Your Child's Concept of Time

Shortly after a ferocious battle during World War II, a soldier was asked what his feelings had been immediately prior to the experience. He responded that he felt he had become suddenly mature because he realized that if he had died, the next day and those thereafter would occur without him. This realization is impossible for a child, whose concept of time is dependent upon their own existence.

Because of a young child's self-centeredness, they cannot conceptualize the universal quality of time: its meaning as the abstraction of all possible sequences of events. Children cannot even conceive of the fact that it is the same day of the week in both their hometown and one nearby. For a young child, time is associated with the concrete events in their life.**4** For example, winter is the time when it snows—whether this snow occurs in January or April.

Children often believe that time is associated with a calendar or a clock and conclude that removing a page from a calendar or advancing a clock will actually make it later. This fantastical aspect of a child's concept of time was perhaps best described by Lewis Carroll who wrote, "... you'd only have to whisper a hint to time, and round goes the clock in a twinkling!"

Confusion in the communication between parents and young children often occurs because children learn time words before they are capable of using them properly. Thus a child may state that they will take their bath at seven o'clock without any sense of actual commitment to performing this activity at that specific time.

"My Child Thinks That I'm An Idiot!"

If one tells youngsters what is really true.
But is not up the greenhorns' avenue,
And then, quite painfully, years hence,
They come to know it at their own expense,
They think they cut it all off their own loaf;
Then they opine their master was an oaf.
Faust (Part II, Act II)
Johann Wolfgang von Goethe

Few parents of teenagers have not had their viewpoints vehemently dismissed because (it was felt) they "don't know anything." And far fewer indeed are the parents who have not become enraged by this assertion. But this belief is not limited only to teenagers: it is also the belief of young children, although they do not verbalize it openly. Why? Are adults as inadequate as their children occasionally believe them to be? Or is this belief necessary for a child's healthy emotional and intellectual development?

Early in their life children consider their parents to be like gods. This belief derives from their dependency on them and from the vast range of parental abilities as compared with a child's. This conviction is essential to the child's development for it enables them to alter their behavior in accord with parental demands, which are also (usually) those of society at large.

But for children to grow and to become independent, for them to change to the degree that they can accept responsibility for their actions, the fiction that their parents are godlike must be destroyed. A child's statements which reject absolutely their parents' knowledge and authority ("Parents are dumb!" "Parents don't know anything!") are intended to help accomplish this change in the child's attitude.

HOW TO BE A LOGICAL PARENT TO YOUR ILLOGICAL CHILD: DO'S AND DON'TS

DO RELAX: THINGS WILL IMPROVE!

It is inevitable that there will be difficulties in communication between parents and children. This derives from their possessing different mental abilities. As the immature mind of your child develops, these difficulties will disappear. This is why many children who experience considerable conflict with their parents during the formative years often establish warm and close relationships with these same parents once they have achieved adulthood.

DO FEEL COMPASSION FOR YOUR CHILD!

Psychological limitations are far more crippling than physical limitations. No parent would request of a child whose leg was broken that they run a hundred yards (or even one yard), but they often demand of this same child that they function in an adult fashion despite their equally severe but "normal" (age appropriate) psychological limitations.

The evolution of the immature mind of a child into the mature mind of an adult is an enormously difficult achievement. The far longer period of dependency for a human child, as compared with the young of other species, is evidence of this.

DO ACCEPT YOUR ANGRY FEELINGS!

It is appropriate to feel angry when one is placed in a frustrating situation. And few situations are more frustrating than when one has difficulty communicating with another person despite the fact that both speak the same language. But you, as a parent, must remember that, although you and your child use the same words, it will require many more years of development for them before you both speak the same language! Acceptance of this fact should help to reduce your feelings of anger when such situations arise.

DON'T CONSIDER YOUR CHILD DIFFICULT FOR "MISUNDERSTANDING" YOUR INSTRUCTIONS!

They can't help it. Occasionally children do covertly defy the demands of their parents by pretending to "misunderstand" their instructions when they fear to defy them openly. But most such instances between parents and (particularly young) children are truly *misunderstandings*.

DON'T THINK THAT YOU CAN TEACH YOUR CHILD THE "ADULT" WAY OF THINKING!

The thinking process of an adult is not something which can be learned: it requires a long period of intellectual evolution. When your child's mind is capable of a mature orientation to events they will have it. Piaget once remarked, with amusement, that the most usual question asked by an American after the orderly evolution of a child's mind has been described to him is, "How can we speed up the process?" Nothing you can do will speed up this process. Unfortunately.

GAZE WITH WONDER AT YOUR CHILD'S BEHAVIOR: IT REFLECTS YOUR MIND AS IT ONCE WAS!

Notes

1. J. J. Gorman, D. G. Cogan, and S. S. Gellis, "An Apparatus for Grading the Visual Acuity of Infants on the Basis of Optico- kinetic Nystagmus," *Pediatrics* 19 (1957): 1088-1092.

2. E. H. Watson, and G. H. Lowrey, *Growth and Development of Children* (Chicago: Year Book Medical Publishers, Inc. 1962).

3. Jean Piaget, *The Origins of Intelligence in Children* (New York: International Universities Press, Inc. 1952), p. 37.

4. O. Grigsby, "An Experimental Study of the Development of Concepts of Relationship in Pre-School Children," *Journal of Experimental Education* Vol. 1 (1932).

CHAPTER FOUR

Of the Sadness and Tasks of Parents

There are are few more difficult times in the lives of parents than when their intuition tells them that the professional advice they are receiving is worthless. Their discomfort is multiplied when they receive the identical questionable advice from several professionals.

Hal was a tall, blond, sixteen-year-old boy. He sat silently in my office as his parents described their concern. Although an excellent student at school and a good worker on his part-time job at a local drive-in, he had few friends. And he had hardly spoken to his parents for the past year. Both the school principal and their family physician had dismissed their concern but they continued to believe that something was wrong.

Hal stared straight ahead as his parents spoke. His face was devoid of emotion. Because he seemed unable to speak in their presence, I asked if he would prefer that we spoke alone. Nodding, and with apparent difficulty, he said, "yes."

We sat in silence for several minutes after his parents had left the room. Hal's body was rigid and he continued to stare. Sensing that he was experiencing a major psychological crisis, I spoke with great deliberation and care. I said, "I realize that you don't know me and don't know yet if you can trust me. But I wonder if despite this you can allow yourself to trust me and tell me what's going on inside of you."

Hal remained rigid while I spoke. When I stopped, his muscles began twitching, first those on his throat, then those on the side of his face. This continued for many moments. Then he gasped, in a hoarse cry, "It's all mixed up!"

With these words our therapeutic collaboration began. But so serious were Hal's conflicts that he was unable to speak to me again for many months. During this period I spoke to him, softly and carefully, until—once more—he was able to risk contact.

The concern which Hal's parents had felt was well justified. It is unlikely that Hal could have avoided hospitalization had they not relied on their intuition about the state of his life and ignored the well-meaning but inaccurate advice given by the several professionals they consulted.

The Carson parents were wonderful people. No other adjective could properly describe them. Art's natural parents had been their neighbors and fellow church members for many years. After they died in an automobile accident, Art had gone to live with Mr. and Mrs. Carson on an informal but permanent basis. They treated him no differently than they treated their own children. And despite the financial burden (for they would not accept government funds for Art's care) and the difficulties which his strange behavior occasioned—behavior far more puzzling than any which they had encountered with their own children—Art was never made to feel anything less than completely welcome in their home. In *his* home.

One Saturday afternoon, upon returning from a visit with relatives (a visit which fourteen-year-old Art had preferred not to join), they discovered that one of their toilets had been painted black with shoe polish. Art accepted responsibility for the deed but was unable to explain this action or his other strange behavior: his refusal to wear the clothing purchased for him by his foster parents, his eating enormous quantities of food when alone in the house, or his purchase of candy with change stolen from Mrs. Carson's wallet.

Several weeks later Art and a schoolmate ran away from home, bound for Florida. They carried with them a change of clothing, some toilet articles, a supply of canned food, and little money. This action caused major concern for the parents of both children: it was midwinter and they lived in the far northern part of the United States. The emotion expressed by the Mr. And Mrs. Carson at our initial meeting was not anger but bewilderment and concern: What was the matter with Art?

Sybil's mother was surprised to learn that her sister had died. So was the sister. They had been eating lunch together when Sybil's schoolteacher arrived to offer condolences for the misfortune which swept the family in recent months: first the illness of Sybil's father, then the death of her grandfather, now the death of her aunt. The teacher understood why Sybil's grades were suffering—at least she thought that she understood until she arrived at Sybil's home.

Although Hal, Art, and Sybil all had psychological difficulties more serious than those which parents usually have to deal with, the feelings experienced by all parents who must attempt to help their child when they are troubled are identical: concern, fear, and anger.

1. *Concern.* There are few emotions more understandable than the concern felt by parents when their child is troubled. A child is far more than a mere relative to their parents who have nurtured him physically and emotionally since birth: the future possibilities in their child's life represent their own longings for a more satisfying existence, and in the child's memory of them is contained the seed of their parents' immortality. Feeling responsible for alleviating their child's distress, yet being unsure of the most helpful course of action, the parents' concern for their child's welfare overshadows virtually all other thoughts in their lives.

2. *Fear.* There are few more unnerving experiences than being confronted by a critical situation about which one has little appropriate knowledge. While most people would

agree with the aphorism that "the mind is a wondrous thing," all would prefer to wonder at the psychological difficulties of others rather than their own. And particularly not those of their children.

An eminent physician has decried the lack of knowledge most people have of their bodies;[1] I would be surprised were research not to reveal that people are in even greater ignorance about the source of their emotions and those of their children.

Early in my treatment of a severely disturbed child it was suggested by her father, a brilliant physician, that increasing the child's intake of caffeine (by drinking coffee) might ameliorate her difficulties.

This absurd suggestion derived not from the man's lack of intelligence nor from any malevolent impulse toward his child. It derived from his attempt to be helpful to a child whose difficulties were equally as mysterious to him as they would be to the least educated member of our society. And the fear which a parent experiences when witnessing the puzzling, often dramatic, and sometimes terrifying behavior of a child when they are troubled is no mean experience. The antidote for this fear is not precipitous action but understanding.

3. *Anger:* To be raised in the United States is to suffer inevitably from the "Father Knows Best" syndrome.* Its major symptoms are the illusions that a child's unhappiness: (a) is of brief duration (although—admittedly —longer than the time between two commercials); (b) is easily understandable (as, Mary is unhappy because she doesn't have a boyfriend); and (c) will disappear spontaneously. Parents often feel angry when their child's periods of unhappiness do not conform to these criteria. They are unaware that their child is not unique in that respect. Thus parents blame themselves for their fantasized "inadequacies" which, they believe, caused the difficulties confronting them, and undeservedly blame their child for their shortcomings which contributed to the situation. But these angry feelings derive from a misinterpretation of the plight they confront.

The parents of Hal, Art, and Sybil sought help for their children because they felt uneasy. They sensed their children's unhappiness. In short, they noticed (although they did not so describe it) a *symptom.*

*I've named this "disorder" after the long-running weekly television series of the 1950s which dramatized "typical" events in the ongoing life of an American family. The creation by television producers of a drama which appeals to the most profound longings in viewers is no small achievement. I treated for many years a severely disturbed teenage boy who passionately enjoyed watching revivals late at night of two television shows: "Father Knows Best" and "The Honeymooners."

The diagnosis of a physical or emotional symptom is not the exclusive province of physicians, psychologists, and other health professionals: this activity is an inextricable part of human life.

Whenever one states they "slept badly" or are "upset" they are making a diagnosis. This diagnosis involves a comparison between their present feelings and what they usually are. Similar judgments are often made about physical objects: Is there a driver who has never observed that "something is wrong" with their car? It is this phrase which precisely defines the term symptom: *a symptom is an indicator of something being "wrong."*

But a particular symptom is not necessarily associated with a specific difficulty! It is the disparity between observable symptom and covert cause, the fact that a particular symptom may reflect any one or a combination of a wide variety of difficulties, that makes a parent's task often seem so formidable. For example, a child's poor grades may reflect: {a) a visual or hearing problem; (b) an inadequate teacher; (c) a covert expression of anger toward their parents manifested by their refusal to behave in accordance with the parents' wishes (by achieving grades which reflect their ability); (d) an unhappy circumstance in their life which interferes with their ability to function.

If the symptom is an intermittent one, it is important to determine when it occurs. Does your child begin biting their nails when they approach the playground or at the arrival of a particular babysitter?

Having once arrived at the house of a divorced friend before the arrival of her babysitter, I spent the next half-hour playing a baseball board game with her nine-year-old son. After leaving the apartment, my friend said, "Bobby was very relieved when he saw which babysitter it was. I don't know why, but he hates the babysitter I've used for the past few weeks." I had not observed Bobby's relief when the babysitter arrived but his mother, because of her years of contact with him, had become aware of the subtle ways in which he expressed emotion.

Because parents are aware of how their child usually behaves, they are able to judge better than a nonprofessional stranger (a teacher or a neighbor) when something is wrong, when a behavior is indeed a symptom of distress. A line in a drama on television provided a good (though apocryphal) illustration of this. An ill child asked his mother if she would hear him if he needed her. Her response was that not only would she hear him if he needed her but that she would hear him if he thought he needed her!

But the determination of which change in your child's life so increased their level of anxiety as to interfere with their healthy development is only the first step in our task. For we must now determine how best to help them.

HOW TO HELP YOUR CHILD WHEN THEY ARE TROUBLED: DO'S AND DON'TS

DO SPEAK TO YOUR CHILD!

Just as gaining knowledge and social contact reduces the discomfort which adults experience when confronting a new and demanding situation, so too does it help a child deal with the crises in their life. A child's life is a lonely and difficult one: it is only the loving concern of their parents which makes bearable their long period of dependency on adults and the long apprenticeship they must serve learning adult ways. Speaking to your child not only reduces their feeling of isolation (for when a child is troubled they have little ability to communicate openly with anyone except their parents) but also increases their belief that your presence and interest in their life are continuous, that you will not suddenly desert them when they need you most, even if they are—at those times—least lovable.

DO ALLOW YOUR CHILD TO "REGRESS"!

When a child is unhappy it is natural for them to act less maturely than they usually do. At those times all of their interest is necessarily devoted to dealing with their unhappiness. Sudden lapses in the maturity of their behavior (for example, more frequent bed-wetting or poorer manners) are temporary: their behavior will become "normal" again when their distress is reduced. To demand that your child retain their customary level of maturity when their life is in crisis is to require more of them than one would of an adult!

DO QUESTION YOUR CHILD
ABOUT THEIR UNHAPPINESS!

Parents sometimes try to avoid speaking of a problem from fear that "talking about it will make it worse." This is unfortunate for their very avoidance does make it worse.

A child senses those topics which their parents spontaneously avoid. When they become aware that their parents are hesitant to discuss the change in behavior, they will conclude not only that their difficulty is too serious for a child to handle but that it is too big for their parents to cope with. This will surely increase the child's feeling of depression for if their parents can't help him then who can?

The most helpful questioning is done not by asking a question but by volunteering a statement for a child may not themselves know why they are unhappy. Thus, rather than ask, "Why are you unhappy?" it is more helpful to say, "I'm concerned. Your father and I feel that you are unhappy but we are just not sure."

Statements such as these do not demand a response from the child but instead grant them the freedom to speak or not as they so wish and to the degree that they desire.

DON'T ASK YOUR CHILD ABOUT THEIR SYMPTOM!

Your child's unhappiness does not derive from their nail biting or nervous tic although his public exhibition of these behaviors may embarrass him. These symptoms reflect the fact that your child is unhappy: they are not the cause of their distress. Your focusing upon the symptom rather than the cause of their unhappiness will make them lose trust in your ability to help them: YOU MAY NOT KNOW THE DIFFERENCE BETWEEN A SYMPTOM AND AN UNDERLYING CAUSE BUT they DO! Moreover, an embarrassing symptom is even more embarrassing (and tends to occur more often) when others pay attention to it.

DON'T SPEAK TO YOUR CHILD ABOUT THE
REACTIONS OF OTHER CHILDREN!

It provides no comfort to your child to be told that another child feels differently about an event (attending school) or an incident (being scolded by a teacher) than they do.

A child's feelings derive from they having incorporated their unique experiences into a comprehensive personality. The parents' task is to help their child mature as an individual so that they will be able to cope with the occasional uncomfortable events and continuous appropriate demands they must face as an adult. This cannot be accomplished by forcing them to graft onto their personality the emotional reactions of another person.

Through observation and discussion (with a child, their teacher, and others) it should be possible to determine what change in a child's life is causing their unhappiness. If the cause is an uncomfortable situation (as, a bully), intervention may be necessary to remedy it. Chapter 5 offers suggestions for helpful ways of intervening. If the source of a child's unhappiness is internal (as, their misconceiving a situation), the most helpful intervention is simply to speak with them about their thoughts and feelings. Suggestions to follow in such a situation are also provided in Chapter 5. Chapter 6 describes those instances in which professional attention is required.

Much of the distress and fear which parents experience when their child becomes unhappy derives from their lacking knowledge of the orderly sequence of events to which the child's periods of unhappiness conform. This sequence can be described in the following few sentences.

A child will inevitably feel unhappy for brief periods during their childhood and adolescence. These periods of unhappiness result from their encounters with various naturally occurring but frustrating experiences.

If a child's unhappiness persists, it is because they are experiencing continuing stress greater than they can tolerate. When this stress disappears, so will their unhappiness.

If the stress is so severe and persistent that it affects their ability to function in important areas of life (as, their school performance), intervention is required to reduce the stress being experienced.

In most situations parental intervention alone will be enough to reduce a child's unhappiness. A few children will require brief professional attention. A far smaller number of children will require extensive professional treatment.

Notes

1. Lewis Thomas, *The Lives of a Cell* (New York: Viking, 1974)

2. J. W. MacFarlane, and M. P. Honzik, *A Developmental Study of the Behavior Problems of Normal Children* (Berkeley. University of California Press, 1954).

CHAPTER FIVE

Key Techniques for Successful Parental Intervention

I often think that the most important effect of parents' intervention is not the actual change they are able to bring about (as their child's placement with a more helpful teacher) but what the child learns from the process of intervention. Perceiving their parents as being able to make changes which improve the quality of their life, a child recognizes that change is possible and that the active struggling against unhappiness is more productive than acquiescence.

A major difficulty for some parents who must decide whether to intervene actively in their child's life is their belief that, like the lone cowboy of innumerable Westerns, a child should fight their own battles. But while the movie cowboy is rarely hurt and usually achieves the prize sought regardless of whatever difficulties are encountered, many children are seriously damaged when they are being forced to struggle alone against impossible odds. And because the damage is internal—psychological—it is often invisible to the child's parents, those who are most concerned with their unhappiness and healthy development.

Most popular myths contain elements of truth. Thus the myth that "a child should fight their own battles" is true, but only when qualified with the words *when a reasonable possibility for their victory exists*. Struggling against insuperable odds is appropriate only when a significant moral or ethical principle is at stake; thus this activity can have significance only for an adult and not for a child.

Parents should not feel guilty or embarrassed when intervening on their child's behalf or demanding that their child's rights be respected. These rights include being provided an effective education, being free from fear of physical violence at school and in the community, and being provided competent medical and psychological treatment when necessary. Because of the complexity of human life, errors of judgment are inevitable, even among the best-trained and most conscientious professionals. But these (and particularly errors due to carelessness) should never be regarded as acceptable.

Many years ago, during my training, I made a minor error in arithmetic while computing a child's intelligence test score. Because of this I appraised it as being two points lower than it actually was. The incorrectly calculated score, while technically an error, had no clinical relevance and viewed from the standpoint of probability theory the two point difference was of no practical significance. But the softly voiced admonition of my supervisor has lingered in my mind ever since. She said, "You do not have the right to make an accidental error when dealing with a patient's life!" She was right. Human life is too important for accidents or shoddy service to be tolerated. Parents should feel anger, not embarrassment, when protesting their child's receipt of inadequate service.

The word intervene derives from the Latin *intervenire* meaning "to come between." When a parent intervenes in the life of their child they are placing themselves between that child and the stressful situation they are encountering, thus protecting him from harm.

This protection occurs even if the intervention is only verbal (for example, speaking with the child about their concern). A child becomes less afraid by identifying with the attitudes of their parents. Perceiving *their* lack of fear (of, say, a frightening dream or a bully), the child begins to question the appropriateness of their own fear of the situation.

Verbal intervention is often all that is needed to reduce a child's distress. Most stresses in a child's life are transient, and aiding a child in these situations may be more necessary for the comfort of the parents than for the healthy development of their child. But although a child's personality is resilient, continual stress will warp its development and reduce the child's ability to realize their intellectual and emotional potential. Thus, verbal intervention is sometimes not enough.

The Rules for Successful Parental Intervention
What *Not to Do* When You Must Intervene
in Your Child's Life

1. **Don't** react too strongly!

Some parents feel so defensive at intervening in their child's life that they act with excessive vigor, so changing the situation that their child's life is now more troubled than before they rendered "aid." An example would be the loud public condemnation of a teacher when their child is disturbed by a bullying classmate. The best intervention in your child's life is that which creates the best effect with the least disturbance. In other words, do the *least* possible!

2. **Don't** intervene directly with another parent's child (*except* in an emergency which contains the potential for serious physical harm)!

Intervening directly with another parent's child will likely cause that parent to intervene angrily with you. Moreover, this action will only provide an example to your child of a fact which they already know: that an adult is more powerful than a child.

3. **Don't** try to protect your child against all possible physical and psychological injuries!

Minor physical injury (as, cuts or bruises) and psychological discomfort derive from a child's need to adjust to their environment and cannot be avoided. But serious physical and psychological damage must be prevented.

QUESTIONS EVERY PARENT SHOULD ASK THEMSELVES BEFORE INTERVENING IN THEIR CHILD'S LIFE

1. Is my intervention necessary? Can my child themselves take the necessary action (as, by asking for help from their teacher in dealing with a class bully)?
2. How can I intervene in such a way that my action will teach my child how to protect their own interests in the future? (Every intervention should both help and educate your child.)

On the following pages several troubling situations common to children are examined in order to illustrate how parents can provide effective intervention.

DO'S AND DON'TS: WHEN YOUR CHILD COMES HOME AFTER A FIGHT

Many parents, when confronted by this situation, rush to act before learning what actually happened because they do not know how to gain this information. But "the facts" can be determined by using one (or more) of the following techniques:

1. **Do** question your child. If you want to know something, ask! Don't be afraid that your interest will arouse anger (or another emotion) in them. If they do get angry (or upset) it means that the occurrence was a more significant event in their life than they first admitted. Thus, the way your child responds to your questions, their words and emotions, convey information equally as important as the facts they assert.
2. **Do** observe your child's demeanor. Are they sulking or composed? Do they seek contact with you (as, by

following you around the house) or does their behavior seem little different from that of a typical day? The greater the difference between your child's behavior and their typical behavior, the greater the effect of the incident upon their life.

3. **Do** tell your child a story. Information is often best acquired indirectly. An example is to tell your child of an incident in your life (or a friend's life) similar to that incident in his life about which you are concerned. Thus you might say, "When I was eight years old I got into a fight and, although no one got hurt, I was awfully scared." If your child is upset about such an incident, hearing your story will encourage them to speak about it.

4. **Do** express your feelings. An example is, "A neighbor told me you were involved in a fight and I was worried you were hurt." Your child will interpret "hurt" to refer to either physical or psychological "hurts" and speak of these if they exist.

These four methods may be remembered by using the acronym QOTE: *Question, Observe, Tell* a story, *Express* your feeling. My ordering of these techniques does not imply that they need be used consecutively or that all be used on any given occasion. Some parents feel more comfortable questioning their child directly; others would prefer to observe their behavior or to tell them a story from their life.

The purpose of these techniques is to help parents obtain the information they need about their child in a manner which is most comfortable for both. For example, questions should not be asked of a child who habitually resents them (as do many adolescents); another technique would provide more information.

These techniques are not "psych-out" methods:* they derive from the earliest history of human interaction and are present in most stable friendships and marriages. By being consciously aware of methods which they have (almost certainly) used automatically for many years, parents can select that technique (or combination of techniques) which, depending upon the emotional state and inclination of their child, proves to be most helpful.

If the child with whom your child had a fight was of their approximate age, if neither was injured seriously, and if your child regards the incident as being "closed," you should not intervene actively. But verbal intervention may still be useful: the passions aroused by even a fight which resulted in no serious consequences can be fearful.

Speaking with your child about their feelings allows them to dissipate and enables your child to integrate this uncomfortable experience into their "theory" of their environment. Mentioning to your child that adults do not (usually) fight, and that there even exist legal penalties for those who do, is helpful. Such statements will reinforce his belief that the environment is not a jungle.

If your child's antagonist was significantly larger or older than them, or if the hostility between them is ongoing, then you must intervene actively to protect your child's happiness and welfare (and, incidentally, those of the other child as well). There are two guidelines which I have found useful in these situations. The first was stated earlier in this chapter. As an adult, your intervention (in any but emergency situations) should be only with another adult.

*This word (in *my* vocabulary) derives from my years of treating a severely disturbed adolescent girl. The word seems to be used most frequently as a verb, as in her statement, "You're trying to psych me out!"

The second rule was expressed (most publicly and in another context) by an American president.* That the most effective intervention is to reason with the parents of the other child: to investigate jointly the dispute between the two children and to arrive at a solution which will be satisfactory for both.

Angry or intemperate threats serve no useful purpose here. They indicate fear and uneasiness rather than strength and clarity of intent. But, more importantly, threats don't work! Even if they are successful in effecting change, the resentment engendered often creates difficulties in the future. Thus it is best, when approaching the parent(s) of your child's antagonist, to say, "It seems like our kids have a problem. What do you think we can do to resolve it?" rather than, "Keep your kid away from mine or else!"

'The well-known injunction of President Lyndon Johnson was to "reason together." Probably no recent president has fostered as much significant legislation designed to advance the psychological and educational development of American children as he.

DO'S AND DON'TS: WHEN YOUR CHILD DOESN'T WANT TO GO TO SCHOOL!

Don't (as is suggested in many child guidance manuals) instantly force them to go to school! The psychological discomfort aroused in your child by this action can be very great.

The major task for a parent is the education and not the control of their child: to provide their child with information and a psychological atmosphere that will allow them to learn from each of their experiences. Although forcing a child to engage in a feared but objectively harmless activity may occasionally be useful (if it causes them to question why they were afraid), the negative consequences can be enormous: causing them to believe that their parents are untrustworthy and unable to understand the degree of terror they experience.

There are, however, effective and safe ways to help a child confront and resolve their fears. Speaking of the situation which they fear helps them to re-experience it gradually, in a more tolerable and gentler form: symbolically through words.

I once treated a young child who greatly feared being alone in a dark room. He would grow upset if he was alone even in a well-lighted room which contained dark corners. In time he told me of the cause of his fears: a creature with the body of a cow and the head and visage of a ferocious lion hid in shadowy corners waiting to devour him.

I never visited the boy's home. I didn't try to reason with his fears. My repeated insistent comment when he described this creature to me was, "It sounds like there are some very scary things going on inside of you!" My statement engendered his emphatic denial, but his fear of dark corners gradually disappeared. It disappeared without my reassurance or pressuring him into confronting it. Because I accepted his feelings and provided him with a theory which placed his fear within a rational perspective (that it represented "some scary things" going on inside of him), he was able to overcome this very troubling experience in his life.

Although every incapacitating physical fear must eventually be confronted (a child who fears going to school or riding in an elevator must eventually do so in order to conquer that fear), experiencing it gradually in verbal (symbolic) form greatly reduces the terror which that final (physical) confrontation occasions.

When a child is afraid to attend school, their parents' initial reaction should be to find out why by using one or more of the four previously described QOTE techniques: Questioning, Observation, Telling a story, Expressing your feeling.

An uncontrollable fear is a symptom indicating that something is wrong. And (as we now know) a symptom should be investigated to determine what is wrong in your child's life. Alleviating your child's unhappiness will cause their symptom to disappear. But forcing the removal of their symptom will not reduce their unhappiness: instead, it will be expressed in another, perhaps more troublesome, manner, or will have a harmful effect upon their psychological development.

What unhappy circumstance can be represented in a child's fear of going to school? It may indicate an upsetting condition at school or a discomfort totally unrelated to their school experience, as, perhaps, their fear of growing up. No valid conclusion can be offered or remedial action prescribed without first obtaining information from your child.

DO'S AND DON'TS: WHEN YOUR
CHILD HAS NIGHTMARES

Most parents first confront this situation early in their child's life. But although nightmares occur most frequently between the ages of four and six years, many older children also experience them: research has revealed that almost one-third of all children aged six to twelve years still have nightmares.1

A nightmare is an intense feeling of fear which occurs during sleep. The child awakens in terror from a dream feeling helpless. While it is most useful to reassure a child at these times, statements like "everybody has bad dreams sometimes" are not helpful. Reassurance which is helpful is that which provides them with a logical perspective within which they can place their troubling experience. Thus a parent might say to a young child (after they have calmed down somewhat), "You know, dreams are really our friends. They tell us what's going on inside of us, what we're really concerned about, but in picture form, like movies. Sometimes these thoughts and feelings can be pretty scary. I wonder what you were worrying about in your dream that was so scary."

Thoughts such as these (when communicated calmly to a child) are helpful because:

1. They confirm your understanding that their experience was truly terrifying, thus increasing the child's confidence in the accuracy of their perception.
2. They provide the child with information about dreams which enables them to react to a nightmare (then and in the future) with reason and understanding.
3. They encourage the child to speak to their parents, to tell them about their uncomfortable experiences. A child's translation into words of their uncomfortable thoughts and feelings reduces the terror they hold: this verbalization enables the child to regard their nightmares as they do the other natural, occasionally fearful, phenomena in their life which are encountered.

DO'S AND DON'TS:
WHEN YOUR CHILD IS USING DRUGS

The phrase "using drugs" is an inexact one. To one parent with whom I had contact it described her teenage son's insistence on drinking two cans of beer while watching a televised football game; to another it reflected her concern over her daughter's use of cocaine.

Any type of drug use should be viewed as indicating a person's attempt to alter their life experience for the better. Whether the drug used is alcohol, a depressant which increases feelings of self-confidence but depresses mental and motor abilities, or amphetamine, a stimulant which creates a feeling of euphoria and enhances (temporarily) both physical and mental abilities, the underlying purpose is identical: to make one feel better.

The parent of every "drug user" should ask themselves two questions:

1. What is my child trying to gain through their "self-medication"?
2. How can I help them to achieve this (relaxation, for example, or relief from anxiety, or an enhanced ability to concentrate) without the use of drugs?

The use of drugs is a symptom and should be approached in the same way as are other psychological symptoms: by investigating your child's life to determine why they are unhappy, and then "prescribing" how their unhappiness may be alleviated. When your child's unhappiness is reduced, so too will their use of drugs.

Parents can discover the cause of their child's unhappiness by using those same QOTE techniques which have been previously described.

Often the terror experienced by parents when their child uses the word drugs (or grass or coke) interferes with their ability to ask the most helpful questions. Fearing superstitiously that to speak about a matter will make it come true (or make it more severe), parents voice their concern circuitously or not at all. Or because they feel inadequate to cope with the situation, they may become authoritarian, ordering their child, "Stop using___! It's upsetting your mother (or father or the whole family)."

My objection to the use of threats by parents does not derive from moral or ethical grounds. My reason for disapproval is a more simple one: threats don't work! Presenting an ultimatum to a child forestalls further discussion and will more likely cause the concealment of the proscribed behavior than its absence, for the underlying unhappiness which produced it will have remained unchanged.

I have yet to meet a child or adolescent who prefers to use drugs, or prefers to obtain grades in school which do not reflect their ability, or prefers that there be conflict in their family. If these conditions exist, it is because the child has little choice in the matter: they are far more unhappy than their parents over the distress in the family, although the smiling or boisterous facade with which they try to conceal this may (unfortunately) so convince their parents (and others) that they will be viewed as a child who is malevolent rather than unhappy.

When parents learn of their child's use of drugs, their questioning should reflect only their desire to obtain information which will enable them to be helpful. Accusations (for example, "How could you do this to your parents?") are neither questions nor are they helpful.

Useful questions include: How long have you been using___? How do you feel about using it? Do you feel its use is interfering with your marks at school? Where do you get the money to buy it? How do you feel we can help you?

These questions are useful because they indicate that you consider the present problem (the use of a drug) as being no different from the earlier difficulties in your child's life. And they will, therefore, expect to receive the same aid and emotional support that you provided in the past.

Despite the occasional blustering of teenagers, their parents remain the major figures of authority for all of their adolescence: attaining complete emotional independence from one's parents occurs, for most people, much later in life.

The "observation" engaged in by parents should provide them with answers to the following questions: Does our child seem upset by their use of drugs? To what degree are these drugs causing a change in their behavior? Was this change present even before they began using drugs? Are they willing to discuss their use of drugs or do they seem to wish to keep the matter "their secret"? Does it seem that they are telling "the truth" or presenting a convenient fiction, one designed to alleviate concern and to forestall active intervention?

The "stories which parents can tell" to their child, both to elicit information from them and to provide them with emotional support, might include their own experiences with addicting substances (cigarettes, alcohol) or activities (eating, gambling), or their own teenage experience of feeling alone as their child does now.

The "emotions which parents can express" include their disappointment at their child not believing they would be accepting and stand by them regardless of the nature of the difficulty they were experiencing, or their wonder at the strength which enabled their child to try to resolve the problem alone for as long as they did.

The use of these four QOTE techniques is designed to elicit the necessary information which will enable parents to proceed to the decisions which will be most helpful to their child and to them. The specific decision cannot be provided within this (or any other) book: human interaction and development is far too complex for there to exist any one solution which will be "correct" for all parents and children. But while the particular decision must depend upon the individual family, the perspective and guidelines provided in these pages concerning those elements which must enter into this decision will be identical for all families. If each family was absolutely unique, the study of human behavior would be impossible.

One significant difficulty experienced by many parents who must help a child "using drugs" is the great anxiety and inaccurate perception which this phrase arouses. Viewing this problem as being qualitatively different from their child's previous difficulties, parents consider themselves without a body of experience, or knowledge, to rely on. They no longer view their child as "a beloved child" but rather as "a drug addict." And, generalizing from their knowledge of other "drug addicts" (gained from the newspapers and novels they read), they now expect their formerly beloved child to be capable of perpetrating the most vile crimes. When a parent's perspective becomes so clouded by fear and misinformation, they are hardly capable of offering aid to their troubled child.

Early one morning I received a telephone call from a woman asking if I treated "children with a drug problem." The drug her daughter, Marta, used was now primarily marijuana; in the past she had used cocaine and LSD. This mother was so blinded by fear of her sixteen- year-old daughter's "drug problem" that she had not observed the grave psychological difficulties which Marta was attempting to alleviate through the use of drugs.

I evaluated the girl that morning. My major concern, after our first moments of contact, was not her use of drugs but the desperate state of her life. Although of good intellectual ability, she had been expelled from several private schools. All the principals' evaluations were similar: Marta was a very bright, very likable girl, but unfortunately, she seemed spontaneously to sabotage her own chance for success in anything she undertook.

Marta was profoundly depressed. Desperately trying to change her life but feeling unable to do so, drugs had seemed her only remaining defense against the impulse toward suicide, the act that would finally release her from a life of torment.

Marta agreed, at the end of her first therapy session, to continue in treatment with me. Her use of drugs diminished considerably within the first few weeks of her psychotherapy. During this period I also established regular (once weekly) contact with her parents, seeking to educate them as to the nature of their daughter's difficulties and to alleviate tension in the family when it arose.

Late one night I received a frantic telephone call from Marta's mother: Marta was demanding $60 to buy marijuana. She said she was an addict and that if her parents did not provide her with the funds necessary to maintain her "habit" she would steal it or obtain it through prostitution. What should they do? I answered that while I would refuse her the money (were I her parent and faced with the need for such a decision), I would not make their decision for them. But I reiterated what I had previously told them: that Marta was not physically addicted to any drugs; that she was terribly unhappy; and that her demand should be viewed, essentially, as that of a "typical teenager": "Give me what I want or else I'll . . ."

Marta's ultimatum was, at least in part, a test of her parents' ability to impose reasonable limits upon her, limits which she too desired. I interpreted her self-description of being "a drug addict" as reflecting her attempt to convey to her parents just how profoundly unhappy she was. Thus she dramatized, for purposes of emphasis, her serious psychological difficulties by using that term (drug addict) which would be most shocking to them. I asked what they would do if Marta had said she was addicted to chocolate chip cookies and demanded money to buy them "or else . . ." They said they would refuse her the money. I suggested that they view Marta's behavior within this context and telephone me again if necessary. My sleep was undisturbed for the remainder of the night.

An adolescent who uses drugs must be viewed primarily as an adolescent who is unhappy about some condition in their life and only secondarily as an "addict." Parents who are unaware that all adolescents experience considerable natural stress and that they may behave and communicate in certain very distinct ways (for example, being moody and having grandiose ideas), are unlikely to be able to help their child resolve their "drug problem."

Marta's father was an eminent economist whose job had demanded that he "provide crucial advice for thirty years." But his lack of knowledge about the nature of emotional difficulties and the natural course of adolescent development rendered him helpless when confronting his daughter's unhappiness.

I should add that the suggestions provided in these past few pages are predicated on the assumption that the child's "drug problem" is not an absolute addiction, that is, that they have some degree of choice about the way they behave. It is this situation which virtually all parents confront. For those very few parents who face a child with virtually no choice about their behavior, professional intervention must be obtained. Suggestions for these parents are presented in Chapter 6.

Do's And Don'ts: When Your Child's Grades Do Not Reflect Their Ability

A common problem hindering parents who try to help a child with academic difficulties derives from the inaccuracy of their perspective: their belief that a child's motivation for learning is imposed from without rather than derived from within. Thus when a child's grades fall the voices of their parents are often raised, as if by increasing the pressure upon their child they could increase the motivation to learn.

But motivation comes from within. And the desire to learn, the craving to develop one's intellectual abilities, is intrinsic to human existence.**2** In the words of Jean Piaget, "The more a child has seen and heard, the more he wants to see and hear.'" Thus parents should view their child's inability to learn in accordance with their abilities as reflecting a symptom, an indication that something is wrong. What is wrong? This can be determined by using the QOTE technique.

Here, questions which are useful include: How do you feel that you are doing in school? Does your opinion agree with that of your teacher? Do you feel you study about as long as the other children in your class? How long have you felt concerned about your schoolwork? Do you feel able to discuss your difficulties with your teacher? If not, why not? Do you feel comfortable in your classroom?

It is also helpful to observe your child's demeanor while questioning them. Do they appear unhappy or puzzled as to why they are being questioned? Do they seem to want to run from the room? Do they become angry as you are speaking and, if so, when? Does their anger appear to reflect discomfort over the subject of your questions or does it perhaps relate to your questioning them insensitively?

Since formal schooling is an experience which all children endure (and have experienced some degree of dissatisfaction with), it should not be difficult for parents to remember their own academic difficulties and to share them with their child. These may have included an incoherent or sadistic teacher, the use of confusing textbooks, or a classmate who insisted on sharing knowledge during an examination.

Sharing these experiences with your child will enable them to use your life perspective in confronting their own difficulty, thereby relieving their distress. Much of the discomfort experienced by children when they are troubled derives from the fact that they have a limited perspective within which to place their present difficulty and therefore do not realize that it will end.

Feelings it would be helpful for your child to hear expressed include your concern and willingness to support them even if this leads to a confrontation with their teacher or the principal of their school. A child will feel less afraid when they realize that they are backed by the power and influence of their parents.

The younger your child, the more probable it is that you will have to intervene directly with their teacher or other school personnel to alleviate the difficulty. The manner in which you approach their teacher will likely determine the degree of your success. If your manner is accusatory, the teacher (particularly if they are inexperienced) will become defensive; and their future interaction with your child may well reflect the anger experienced (but not expressed) toward you.

A parent should keep in mind three goals when meeting with the teacher of their child: (1) to determine the nature of their child's difficulty, (2) to formulate a plan to remedy the difficulty, and (3) to motivate the teacher to want to help the child.

The third goal is equally as important as the first two. It is crucial to establish a friendly relationship between teacher and parent so that the teacher will extend themselves to help the child with their difficulty.

Because school has so great an influence on a child's life—providing them with the opportunity to acquire, utilize, and test their social and intellectual skills—emotional difficulties are often reflected first in school difficulties. These school difficulties may be academic, social, or disciplinary in nature.

Thus a child's difficulty in learning algebra may reflect emotional aspects of their personality: the fear that, were they to permit their mind to range freely (as is required for the successful solution of an algebra problem), they would discover much about their life experience that they prefer not to be aware of. And a child's continual fighting with their peers may reflect a displacement of the anger they feel toward themselves at the unsatisfactory state of their life.

Often a child's cry for help goes unrecognized. I sometimes tell the following incident from my own life to my adolescent patients. Because I was the tallest (and most obedient) child in my second grade class, I was seated in a far corner of the room. Bill, slightly shorter, sat directly in front of me. Each day after the distribution of the index cards on which practice arithmetic problems were printed, several were surreptitiously torn into small pieces and placed in an empty desk next to Bill—and me. After several days the pieces were discovered. The teacher's response was predictable: she warned Bill that his outrageous behavior must stop. Bill, expressing bewilderment, protested his innocence as I sat quietly with a righteous expression on my face.

The empty desk continued to fill with torn index cards and the teacher's anger grew; she repeatedly warned Bill that if he did not stop this disgraceful behavior she would call his mother to school. Bill's vociferous protestations of innocence only increased the teacher's wrath. Finally, she carried out her threat.

The next day Bill's mother accompanied him to school. I sat, apparently immersed in my arithmetic lesson, and listened to their conversation: the bewilderment of Bill's mother, his protestations of innocence, the teacher's anger. One of the teacher's statements was particularly loud: "Only two students could have done this, Stanley and Bill, and Stanley would never do anything like this!"

Calling Bill's mother to school proved to be that move which resolved the problem. The destruction of arithmetic cards ended. The sight of Bill's mother in school had so frightened me that I found another way to express my anger at the unhappiness in my life.

Do's And Don'ts: When Your Child Masturbates in Public!

There is really no cause to be concerned when your child rubs their genitals in public. They, being logical, can perceive no difference between caressing their genitals and touching any other part of their body. This practice usually diminishes during the toddler years when a child acquires the behavior patterns appropriate to children in American society. When masturbation persists beyond the toddler years (that is, if it occurs so frequently as to be noticeable), it usually indicates that the child is unhappy.*

Because it is pleasurable, a child's frequent masturbation reflects their attempt to compensate for their unhappiness. It also reflects their attempt to regress to an earlier, happier period in their life, that period when the open touching of their genitals was more acceptable.

The child's unhappiness may derive from: the birth of a sibling which arouses anger (because of the reduction in parental attention this event has caused) that they fear to express openly; the actions of a sadistic babysitter; sexual overstimulation caused by repeated bathing with a parent; or their response to a psychologically traumatic medical procedure involving their genitals. When the child's unhappiness diminishes, so too will this behavior.

* I am assuming, of course, that the cause of this behavior is not underclothing that is too tight or the presence of a skin inflammation.

My goal in this chapter has not been to advise parents as to rigid ways of responding to their child's problems. My objective has been to provide helpful guidelines for parents to follow when intervention in their child's life is indicated. These guidelines derive from my perspective on human development and change, a viewpoint which I have found useful in helping innumerable children and their parents.

While there are countless situations in which a parent's active intervention is appropriate, my viewpoint concerning intervention in situations other than those specifically discussed (school difficulties, drug problems, and the like) can be summarized in the following few statements:

1. Be sure that you understand the primary causes of your child's unhappiness before you intervene in their life.
2. A parent's obsessive worrying never improves their child's life: thinking does.
3. There are very few situations in a child's life (apart from medical emergencies or major psychological crises) when several minutes cannot be spared for thoughtful consideration before action is taken.
4. RELAX! RELAX! RELAX!

These four statements may be further compressed into the following three words: THINK AND RELAX.

Helping Yourself Relax When Your Child Is Troubled: The Method of Self-Hypnosis

Relaxation is not synonymous with disinterest. Parents can be most helpful to their troubled child when they are able, deliberately and temporarily, to remove themselves from involvement with their child, returning after a period of relaxation with (perhaps) an altered perspective on the situation.

But how? Does there exist a technique for relaxation which is completely safe, drug-free, natural for the human body, and inexpensive? Absolutely! So natural is this technique that it is used routinely by newborn infants—by themselves.

When an infant experiences an uncomfortable and unavoidable provocation (like a loud, continual noise), they succeed in tolerating the discomfort by becoming deeply relaxed: their physical movements are reduced and the measurements obtained from recordings of their respiration and the electrical activity of their brain parallel those obtained when they are sleeping deeply. When the uncomfortable stimulus disappears, the infant spontaneously "awakens" and returns to their usual very active state.[4]

The autonomic changes observed in these infants are similar to those found in adults who have learned the techniques of self-hypnosis.[5] So powerful are the effects of these techniques (or, more accurately, of the bodily processes which they can foster) that they have been used successfully to treat such disparate conditions as warts,[6] sleepwalking in an adult,[7] asthma,[8] obesity,[9] and migraine headache.[10] They have been successful (improbable though it may seem) in crime detection,[11] and the stimulation of breast growth in adult females.[12,13] Their use has even been suggested as a method for controlling the blood flow to cancerous tumors.[14] These techniques have been so effective in easing tension and relieving pain that they have even been taught to children and adolescents dying of cancer.[15]

While the use of hypnosis for a specialized purpose (such as reducing pain, losing weight, treating asthma) requires extensive training and knowledge, its use solely for relaxation demands no more than that a person assist the induction and course within themselves of a completely natural process.

THE PROCEDURE FOR SELF-HYPNOSIS

1. Lie down on a bed or couch in a quiet room. While absolute quiet may be impossible to attain, the presence of slight noises will not be a hindrance. If possible, the telephone should be disconnected to avoid interruption. Clothing should be loosened and contact lenses or eyeglasses removed.

2. As you're lying on the couch relaxing comfortably, close your eyes and begin to breathe deeply, Don't hold your breath or do anything which feels unnatural or uncomfortable: merely take several deep breaths while attending to the rhythm of your breathing.

3. After several moments of deep breathing, relax the muscles of your body, beginning with those in your forehead. Thus, as you lie comfortably on the couch, concentrate first on the muscles of your forehead and relax them. Then focus on the muscles about your cheeks and relax them. (The relaxation of particular muscles is not experienced as a sudden jarring sensation: the feeling is more akin to a gentle "letting go.") After the muscles about your cheeks are relaxed, concentrate on those about your mouth. Progressively concentrate on and relax each group of muscles in your body from your forehead through your toes, paying attention, in sequence, to all parts of your body: your head, your chest and pelvic area, your arms and hands, and your legs and toes.

4. When all of your muscles are completely relaxed, begin thinking of a comfortable scene. This may be lying on the sand at a beach with a comfortable breeze blowing over your body or relaxing on the grass in the country. Don't visualize a scene at which a painful event

occurred (for example, lying on a beach if you once became severely sunburned at a beach). As you continue to visualize the scene, try to immerse yourself in it. Think (if the scene is at a beach) of the warmth of the breeze on your body and try to feel it. Try to feel the warmth of the sand under your body and to hear the sound of the waves rolling onto the shore.

5. Lie like this for several minutes. Then, very gradually, remove your thoughts from the soothing scene you have visualized, open your eyes, and begin to move your arms and legs. Do this in a leisurely manner and wait several minutes before getting up.

This self-hypnotic technique will not remove the difficulties confronting your child. But after the temporary relief from your stress, you will be better able to help your child. Part of the discomfort experienced by parents when their child is troubled derives from their inability to cease the continual, unproductive, painful worrying which envelops them.

With knowledge of the techniques described in this chapter and the perspective on child behavior and development provided in this and previous chapters, parents should be able to work together with their child to alleviate most situations which trouble them. But, at times, some children do develop difficulties which can only be reduced or eliminated through professional intervention. Chapter 6 describes the nature of these difficulties and how to obtain competent, cost-effective treatment for them.

1. R. Lapouse and M. A. Monk, "Fears and Worries in a Representative Sample of Children," *American Journal of Orthopsychiatry* 29 (1959): 803-818.

2. J. McV. Hunt, "Piaget's Observations as a Source of Hypotheses Concerning Motivation," *Merrill-Palmer Quarterly* 9 (1963): 263-275.

3. J. Piaget, *The Origins of Intelligence in Children* (New York: International Universities Press, 1952), p. 276.

4. T. B. Brazelton, "Observations of the Neonate," *Journal of the American Academy of Child Psychiatry*, 1 (1962): 38-58.

5. L. C. Walrath and D. W. Hamilton, "Autonomic Correlates of Meditation and Hypnosis," *American Journal of Clinical Hypnosis* 17 (1975): 190-197.

6. T. A. Clawson, and R. H. Swade "The Hypnotic Control of Blood Flow and Pain: The Cure of Warts and the Potential for the Use of Hypnosis in the Treatment of Cancer," *American Journal of Clinical Hypnosis* 17 (1975): 160-169.

7. T. S. Eliseo, "The Hypnotic Treatment of Sleepwalking in and Adult," *American Journal of Clinical Hypnosis* 17 (1975): 272-276.

8. G. P. Maher-Loughnan, "Hypnosis and Autohypnosis for the Treatment of Asthma," *International Journal of Clinical and Experimental Hypnosis* 18 (1970): 1-14.

9. J. H. Aja, "Brief Group Treatment of Obesity through Ancillary Self-Hypnosis," *American Journal of Clinical Hypnosis* 19 (1977): 231-234.

10. L. K. Daniels, "Treatment of Migraine Headache by Hypnosis and Behavior Therapy: A Case Study," *American Journal of Clinical Hypnosis* 19 (1977): 241-244.

11. H. C. Salzberg, "The Hypnotic Interview in Crime Detection," *American Journal of Clinical Hypnosis* 19 (1977): 255-258.

12. R. D. Willard, "Breast Enlargement through Visual Imagery and Hypnosis," *American Journal of Clinical Hypnosis* 19 (1977): 195-200.

13. A. R. Stain and D. R. Logan, "Hypnotic Stimulation of Breast Growth," *American Journal of Clinical Hypnosis* 19 (1977): 201-208.

14. Clawson and Swade, "Hypnotic Control of Blood Flow and Pain," *American Journal of Clinical Hypnosis,* 17 (1975): 160-169.

15. C. Holton, K. Tewell, and D. Eccles, "The Use of Self-Hypnosis by Children with Cancer," *American Journal of Clinical Hypnosis* 17 (1975): 233-238.

CHAPTER SIX

When Parents Are Not Enough:
Of Professional and
Unprofessional Treatment

The Lost Pleiad

I met her again in Boston. She was still very lovely. Was this why I spoke to her? Or was it my delight at meeting an old friend again after seventeen years? Or perhaps it was my loneliness, that emotion endemic to a lonely participant at a convention, living in a hotel surrounded by couples. And so I spoke to her and heard a story which I would, perhaps, have preferred never to have learned: the story of her life.

She had majored in mathematics at college and then achieved a graduate degree in chemistry. While still in graduate school she had been involved in a major scientific discovery, and her photograph had appeared in several newspapers. After graduation she was hired by a large multinational corporation. Several years later she was selected for inclusion in Who's Who.

When I met Ingrid that day in Boston she had been out of work for eight years. During this period she had been hospitalized in two psychiatric institutions. The first hospitalization was voluntary and had been suggested by the medical staff of the corporation where she worked. Her second hospitalization occurred when a policeman found her very early one morning, seated and crying in the street.

For most of these eight years Ingrid had lived with and been supported by her mother. Her mother died recently and Ingrid now lived alone in her mother's apartment, supported by funds from an inheritance. Her days were spent lying in bed or walking through the streets of the city.

Ingrid occasionally practiced fencing: her mother had won a medal for fencing in the 1936 Olympics and Ingrid studied the sport since childhood. Her only companions were widows her mother had befriended; the youngest was thirty-five years older than Ingrid.

Ingrid dated infrequently, attempting to follow the advice of her most recent therapist who counseled her to marry and supplied her with tranquilizing medication. Thus Ingrid's life had become like that of the mythical Lost Pleiad, the daughter of Atlas who hid herself from shame and grief.

Ingrid told me much of this story while we sat in her apartment, surrounded by her mother's heavy, antiquated furniture. I sat with Ingrid and drank her coffee, read her listing in Who's Who and looked at her old photograph in the newspapers she had saved. Before I left, I tried to help her in the only way I knew how: by imploring her to contact a very gifted colleague for treatment. I telephoned him that day. I telephoned him again several weeks later: she had not contacted him. Months later when I returned to Boston I called Ingrid. Her phone rang for half a minute. Then the receiver was picked up and, wordlessly, dropped back into place.

I think of Ingrid often, wondering why her life became as it had. I knew her slightly at college: we shared a class together. I remember her saying then, somewhat disappointed, that the men in her classes treated her like a sister. And that afternoon as she spoke in her apartment, I sensed her fear of closeness and wondered if she were not, at thirty-six years of age, still a virgin. Perhaps years before, her classmates too had sensed her ambivalence about intimacy and responded to her accordingly.

Should I have been more friendly to her at college? Could I have been more of a friend to her in Boston?

Probably my persistent comparison between her present fearful existence and her puzzled frown at age nineteen derive from my sense of horror at the destruction of her enormous potential, my vision of how her life might have been. Some may feel, as Sophocles said in the last lines of Ajax, that

> *What men have seen they know;*
> *But what shall come hereafter*
> *No man before the event can see,*
> *Nor what end waits for him.*

But those who have been scarred by serious emotional conflict and violated by ineffectual treatment have little hope for joy or fulfillment in their lives. Their "end" will almost surely be unhappy.

Often the effects of early emotional conflict and damage accrue through childhood, becoming noticeable only when the magnitude of unhappiness, no longer able to be contained, is expressed in that startling behavior and speech which society has come to characterize, colloquially, as "being crazy," and, professionally, with such classifications as (for Ingrid) Schizophrenia, Paranoid Type, 295.30 in DSM-IV.*

Situations containing the seeds from which serious emotional difficulties arise demand professional psychological intervention. Frequently a child will develop a symptom which, because it reflects their experience of a temporary stressful situation, will soon disappear without intervention.

"DSM-IV is the fourth edition of the Diagnostic and Statistical Manual of Mental Disorders. The 295 category (295.10, 295.20, and so on) classifies the schizophrenic disorders.

If the stress (and therefore the symptom) persists, help provided by their parents, using the methods and having the perspective described in this book, should alleviate it. If, however, a child's discomfort still persists despite the efforts of his parents, then professional psychological intervention should be sought. How can parents be sure to recognize these situations? Simply by paying attention to their feelings. When their feeling of unease continues, when they feel that they are no longer able to affect their child's behavior, that the situation in their child's life is out of their control, then they should seek professional intervention.

This intervention need not be prolonged particularly if the child's difficulty has not persisted too long. Often providing parents with a different perspective on their child's difficulties suffices to enable them to help their child themselves. But when a child has experienced a stressful situation for a considerable period its effect persists even after the removal of the situation. The stressful situation has then become "internalized," has gained an autonomous life of its own in the child's theory of their environment, and this effect is remediable only through psychotherapy. This is not remarkable since prolonged (or even temporary) severe stress has long been known to warp the development even of psychologically healthy adults.

Psychotherapy: The Treatment of the Mind

What is psychotherapy and how does it work? Psychotherapy is a technique for treating emotional difficulties. Although it consists of speech between two people, it is not conversation. Those clinicians who chatter with their patients under the guise of treatment do a disservice to their patients and their profession. While, infrequently, a therapist may speak with their patient of matters identical to those discussed between friends (as, the weather or a popular novel), their purpose in discussing these matters is always different: the psychological growth of their patient.

Every word that a psychotherapist utters must have only one goal: the treatment of their patient's mind. If this is not the case then the patient is receiving less effective treatment than they should. Much of the confusion experienced by parents who seek treatment for their child (or themselves) derives from the current broadening of the original meaning of the term psychotherapy and the inadequate training of far too many current "therapists."

The term psychotherapy originally referred to the method devised by Sigmund Freud for treatment of a particular kind of emotional disturbance, a neurosis. This treatment involved very frequent (usually daily) contact between therapist and patient, the latter reclining on a couch and speaking their uncensored thoughts. The therapist's task was to study their patient's words and to help them make logical connections between their sometimes fearful thoughts and feelings and the understandable desires they symbolized. This procedure was intended to reduce the patient's feeling of terror and to restore their mental equilibrium.

Many myths prevail about this method. The most popular depicts the silence of the therapist as being so continual that the patient sometimes wonders whether they are even awake. While a few present practitioners may confuse an occasionally useful technique (silence) with the method of treatment, Freud himself never did. The eminent psychoanalyst, Heinrich Racker, has described as extremely varied and creative the manner in which Freud participated with his patients. He describes Freud as almost continually engaging the patient in a dialogue, often illustrating his comments with quotations from classical literature.[2]

Before we can understand the nature of psychotherapy as it relates to children, we must again return to our earlier analysis of how a child's mind develops, for the only goal of a child's psychotherapy is the healing of their mind. Those changes which both parents and children desire—an increased capacity for learning, greater self-control, more "understandable" behavior, and so on—can derive only from the attainment of this goal.

As we have seen, the child spontaneously creates a theory of their environment which enables them to fulfill their needs more effectively than if they had, each moment, to rediscover the nature of their world. This theory includes many "facts" concerning the objects they encounter (as, their rattle, ball, crib, a toy, and so on).

But people too are *objects* to the child, and thus theories about them are also created based upon the "facts" which the child experiences. But because a child's mind is immature and, until adolescence, is unable to evaluate their theories properly, they may develop inaccurate theories about themselves, their parents, and their environment.

And because a child's behavior is based upon their perception of the world, which is encapsulated in their theories of its nature, these inaccurate theories will gravely hinder their ability to function adequately, and will cause them to behave in ways which interfere with rather than aid their ability to satisfy themselves.

These inaccurate theories may include such "facts" as that they are unlovable, that they are ugly, that they are stupid, that they cannot learn anything properly, that the world is malevolent, and, of course, innumerable others.

Believing any of these "facts" causes great discomfort. For example, a child who believes they are unlovable will tend to avoid contact with other people because they will expect to be rejected. Thus their life will be devoid of warmth, which can only be obtained through intimacy with others.

Why does a child tend to retain, uncorrected, those of their theories which are inaccurate? For the same reason that roads are more often repaired than replaced: because of the great difficulty and cost involved.

A child's theories about their basic nature and that of their environment (including the people who inhabit it) are formed early in their life and serve as the bedrock of their personality, the firm foundation which underlays all their activities. Were the child to reject these they would have no stable perspective from which to interpret their experience and to interact with the world.

It is the terrifying and pervasive fear that occurs when one has no rational structure within which to understand and order their experiences that is communicated in the word *madness*. Rather than experience this, the child with an inaccurate perspective will distort their experiences to fit their existent theory rather than to reject it.

If the child (or adolescent) is able to function adequately in school, if their experience of events (of "reality") is largely undistorted, and if their symptoms are primarily troublesome thoughts and fears and feelings of anxiety, then their difficulty is described technically as a *neurosis*.

If a child's difficulties are so severe that they are unable to function in all areas of their life, if they have little commitment to judging events with regard to their actuality, if their emotional response to events is grossly different from that reflected by others, and if their speech is often difficult to understand, then the child's difficulties are described as *psychotic* (or reflecting a *psychotic disorder* or a *psychosis*).

If the child experiences little anxiety, exhibits few neurotic symptoms, is able to judge reality effectively but nevertheless acts according to a deeply ingrained pattern of behavior which interferes with their attainment of those satisfactions they most need, then they are said to possess elements of a *character disorder*.

If a child's psychological stress so interferes with their bodily functioning that physical changes occur (certain cases of peptic ulcer, ulcerative colitis, bronchial asthma, and so on), then they are said to suffer from a *psychophysiologic* (or *vegetative*) disorder.

These four psychological disorders (neurosis, psychosis, character disorder, psychophysiologic disorder) are internalized: they reflect conflict (or its partial resolution) between different parts of the child's mind: their attempt to satisfy their needs while retaining their "inaccurate" theory, and, with psychotic disorders, a distortion in the development of those mental functions which are involved in speech, thought, individuation, feeling, and perception. The child whose difficulties fall within the limits of any of these four disorders can only be healed through psychotherapy.

This categorization has necessarily been simplified: psychological disorders do not occur in categories as neat as these. True character disorders rarely occur before late adolescence, nor true neurotic disorders before, approximately, five years of age. Most children exhibit combinations of symptoms: to diagnose accurately one must speak of the neurotic, characterological, and, possibly, psychotic elements in their personality, although one category may so dominate that a child's difficulties are often described as reflecting a neurotic or psychotic disorder.

When a professional speaks of *psychopathology* they refer primarily to these four conditions although other categories such as brain syndrome (the impairment of mental functions caused by damage of the brain, particularly cerebral cortex tissue, do exist.

Parents of Emotionally Disturbed Children: Guilty or Not Guilty?

For years I met bimonthly with a small group of parents whose adolescent children were hospitalized for emotional disturbance. These children were profoundly disturbed: several had required treatment before they were old enough to attend grade school. Over the course of our years of contact every parent said, in one way or another, "I feel guilty because my child is like they are." My response in each instance was to state that our task was not to assess guilt but to determine how to help their child change. (My statement was not directly responsive to their expressed feeling. To have been directly responsive would have required that the group meet more frequently and demanded a change in its nature, changes which were impossible to effect.)

Was the guilt felt by these parents justified? Why do some children develop difficulties while others remain unscathed?

Each child is an individual. Each possesses a certain temperament which may be easier or more difficult to parent, and an inborn capacity to develop psychological (ego) defenses, ways of protecting themselves when they experience stress. For example, the child described in Chapter 5 who feared dark corners nevertheless functioned well in school. Because he was able to encapsulate his difficulties so that they affected relatively small and unimportant areas of his life (that is, when he was in a room with a darkened corner), he was able to protect himself against the major stress he was experiencing. Had he not been able to do this, his life would have become increasingly disorganized, perhaps so disorganized that a diagnosis of psychosis would have been appropriate.

All parents cannot be effective caretakers to all children, nor can all children experience, undamaged, all manner of stress. Nor is the same nurturing experience appropriate for all children: what is too intense for one because of his temperament, is too little for another.

While some family settings are so conflicted that virtually no child could experience them unscathed, no parents deliberately harm their child: they aid their development as best they can given the personality limitations they themselves have derived from their own childhood experiences and the concurrent external stresses in their lives.

For example, if a mother was reared to believe that physical closeness, self-assertion, or the open expression of feelings are "bad," she will have difficulty raising a child who believes otherwise. And even if she deliberately forces herself to act freer, her child, with that sensitivity granted to all children, will sense how their mother unconsciously wants them to behave, and will act accordingly. Thus the child will grow to maturity fearing physical closeness, self-assertion, or the expression of feeling, as does their parent.

Should I have permitted those parents to continue to condemn themselves for their inevitable mistakes as parents?

THE DYING FATHER

I once was referred several children by their father, who was dying of cancer. He entrusted them to me for treatment in his last year of life. When we spoke, despite his illness, it was of his concern for them. He had always feared intimacy and, having spent his life searching for and achieving financial success, he had avoided experiencing many of those emotions which provide life with meaning. And he fostered similar difficulties in his sons.

I have never doubted that the emotional difficulties developed by his children reflected, at least partially, the "mistakes" he had made as a parent. But I remember too his leaving his hospital bed the night before surgery and returning home to comfort his sick child. During his last years he had struggled to change his life, to find love and warmth and closeness. But we spoke little about his life in those months and weeks before his death. Instead we discussed his concern for his sons, of his desire that they achieve a more satisfying life than he had.

He spoke of his girl friend with compassion and understanding, and of his children with puzzlement and understanding and love. He allowed himself no delusions during this period: he knew that he was going to die. But he struggled mightily against it. His last hours were spent making business decisions and comforting his children and his girl friend. And when he died his ex-wife, his girl friend, and his children wept. And together they spread his ashes on the earth at the home in Virginia which he had loved so well.

My experiences with parents of emotionally disturbed children have convinced me that there are few who have not felt that

> *. . . everything I touch*
> *Is dust, and death*
> *has leapt upon my life.**

Any further instilling of remorse in these parents, by elaborating on their "errors," would indeed be cruel.

---

* Creon in Sophocles' *Antigone*.

My experience as a clinician has included patients ranging in age from four through seventy years, patients both in and out of hospital settings, children and adolescents who were functioning well or inadequately, adults of various professions and no profession and those who were unemployed. I cannot remember the eye color of any of these people, am certain of the hair color of only two, and have a vague sense of the height of several. But I well remember the gist of my contact with each, the nature of their difficulties, and the varying therapeutic approaches I adopted with each and why.

Which is to say that the task of a psychotherapist is to relate to internal (psychological) and not external phenomena: they work inside of the patient's mind. Those psychotherapists who view their only task as being to provide their patient with advice, or to encourage their expression of feelings, or to chat are not, despite their use of the word, providing *psychotherapy*. Such activity may, with selected individuals, be helpful, but it is not healing.

I once was consulted by the divorced mother of two children, a ten-year-old girl and a four-year-old boy. She had been taking them to a "therapist" whose goal was to encourage both children to verbalize their "angry feelings." The sessions consisted mainly of the girl expressing her "angry feelings" toward her brother. Understandably, the boy was growing more and more nervous, vehemently refusing to attend further "therapy" sessions. This clinician's ignorance of the nature of human development and psychotherapy caused this mother to engage her children in such activity that each was deteriorating psychologically.

Her naiveté caused her to act on the inaccurate premise that psychotherapy consisted of encouraging the ventilation of feelings rather than to understand that this is but one tool of a psychotherapist and one which should be used only with great caution and after much deliberation.

Thus this clinician was harming and not helping these patients.

The task of a psychotherapist is to assess the nature of their patient's difficulties, those emotional conflicts and (occasionally) ego limitations* which derive from inadequate childhood experiences, and to provide them with that particular interpersonal experience which will allow them to become healed. This assessment (diagnosis) is complex. It demands that one be familiar with all of a patient's mental capacities and know how best to interact with them on a moment-to-moment basis so that the healing of each of these capacities is fostered and their mind becomes healed. Thus prolonged psychotherapy is not required by a child or adult whose difficulties reflect their experience of a temporary stress. These reactive disorders (that is, difficulties which are *reactive* to a temporary troubling situation) will disappear when the precipitating stress does. Brief supportive psychotherapy may be helpful to alleviate the discomfort, but it is usually not essential.

*The ego is that hypothesized part of the mind which acts as mediator between a person's desires and their environment. It is not tangible and consists of processes, not a physical organ or tissue. These processes perform various functions: providing a person with self-awareness; enabling them to assess the reality of their experience; providing them with memory, the ability to control their feelings, the ability to reconcile their conflicting desires, and other capacities. Thus the term ego limitations refers to a person with an inadequate capacity to perform one or more of these functions, such as assessing the reality of their experience, and so on. Jon G. Allen, Ph.D., provided an excellent summary and clarification of thinking about the nature and development of the ego in the *Bulletin of the Menninger Clinic* (November, 1977).

The Four Basic Ways a Psychotherapist Interacts with Their Patient

There are four psychotherapeutic postures, four ways in which a therapist facilitates the healing of their patient's mind. These are the *analytic posture,* the *supportive posture,* the *relationship posture,* and the *replacement posture.* Each word that a therapist speaks reflects their decision as to which one (or combination) of these postures to use. The therapist's ability to assess—at each moment—the mental and emotional state of a patient and to determine the most healing statement or question is what makes the practice of psychotherapy so difficult and what requires extensive academic education and clinical training. A psychotherapist acts sometimes as a friend, sometimes as a scientist, and sometimes as a nurturing figure. But they are always a healer.

The therapist's role when they adopt an analytic psychotherapeutic posture is that of a "scientist-human being," one who, with warmth and acceptance, works together with their patient to analyze the patient's life experiences. The therapist's goal is that the patient change so that, eventually, links are established between their previously feared thoughts and feelings and their childhood experiences, and their present theory of their life comes to incorporate these previously discomforting events.

While the therapist makes some interpretations of these thoughts and feelings which are more useful than others, none can be absolutely true. This is both impossible and irrelevant. It is impossible because no person can ever know another entirely; and it is irrelevant because it is the joint process of interpretation which is healing, not any particular interpretation.[3] The primary function of an interpretation is to provide the patient a rational organizing structure within which to incorporate their experiences.

When the therapist adopts a supportive psychotherapeutic posture they attempt to act as an ideal helper, analogous to a fireman engaged in rescuing the inhabitant of a burning building. The therapist provides advice and occasionally involves themselves in their patient's environment outside of the office in order to strengthen the patient's present ability to cope with those stresses which are impinging upon them. When interpretations are made these tend to be superficial.

When the therapist adopts a relationship psychotherapeutic posture they attempt to behave as would an ideal friend: to act in such a manner that the patient can, temporarily, satisfy their need for a person toward whom they can express both tender and hostile feelings.

But this relationship must always remain strictly verbal: for a therapist to allow their patient's yearnings to be acted out physically would be destructive to the lives of both and would mark the end of the healing process. It is inevitable that a therapist occasionally become aroused sexually by one of his (or her) patients, but the absolute prohibition against intimacy between them serves to protect both patient and therapist.

Equally necessary is the prohibition against physical harm to oneself, another person, or to property. Effective psychotherapy is not possible when the therapist is concerned for their own safety (or their patient's safety or the intactness of the office). While some possibility of physical harm always exists when treating profoundly disturbed patients, its occurrence usually reflects a mistake made by the therapist. That colleague in my experience who suffered the greatest number of physical attacks from teenagers (a broken rib, a broken finger, other "serious" punches) tended to assert himself with patients before he was sufficiently knowledgeable about the situation. But not always does an injury reflect an error. I had another colleague who always sat in the hospital dining room with his back to the wall, facing the center of the room: many years before, while he was a psychiatric resident, a patient had walked over to a colleague with whom he was speaking and, without warning, had punched him so severely that his jaw was broken. The injured doctor was a stranger to the patient.

The replacement psychotherapeutic posture is necessary with the most severe psychological difficulties. Here the therapist attempts to act as an ideal mother, their goal being to heal the patient's deficient ego functions. When a therapist uses this posture they must be continually available to their patient; ideally there should be no moment of the day when the therapist cannot be contacted.

One very dedicated colleague was asked by his daughter if his next vacation would again be a "telephone vacation" because on his last holiday he had spent several hours daily speaking, by telephone, with the very psychologically damaged patients he treated. Another colleague received two to three telephone calls each day for several years from one particular patient.

In such cases, frequent contact is necessary because patients with ego deficiencies often have an inadequate sense of their own continuity as a person and of the continuous existence of the therapist to whom they are entrusting their life for healing. Thus, frequent contacts alleviate the anxiety which these patients experience when, intermittently, they become possessed by the fear that they —or the therapist—no longer exist. When using this posture the therapist, like an ideal mother, must verbally attempt to satisfy all the longings of their patient; and those psychological demands which they make of the patient (as, that they exhibit a degree of trust in a relationship) must not be beyond the patient's ability to perform (for an individual with severe psychological difficulties often possesses very little capacity to trust another).

Often unconventional and ill-trained therapists, unaware of the complexities of human development, attempt to satisfy unsatisfied childhood yearnings by prescribing to an adult who experienced an unsatisfactory parenting experience that they be held in the therapist's arms or drink from a baby bottle or eat baby food. These therapists fail to understand that the experience which can satisfy the longings of a child when they are a child is not the identical experience which can satisfy these yearnings when the patient is an adult.

It is because of the difficulty in determining the equivalent experience required to heal an adult whose ego functions have been damaged as the result of a severely destructive childhood, and because of the extensive time required for treatment that would replace these functions with more adequate ones, that such patients have been relegated, primarily, to treatment with powerful tranquilizing drugs, some of which have horrendous side effects.* Or they may be granted only cursory treatment, such as bimonthly "maintenance" psychotherapy.

* Alan Stone, M.D., Professor of Law and Psychiatry at Harvard University, believes that ". . . enormous malpractice liability will begin to accrue over the next decade because of cases of tardive dyskinesia secondary to neuroleptic drugs." Tardive dyskinesia is a drug side effect causing involuntary muscular contortions of the face, mouth, lips, and tongue.' The great number of possible lawsuits may be imagined by realizing that millions of American children and adults have been treated with these drugs: one phenothiazine drug, chlorpromazine, ranked thirty-third in a list of the 200 most widely used psychotropic drugs·[6] Despite the widespread use of these drugs there is serious question as to their effectiveness. David Marholin II and David Phillips have provided an excellent critique of current research·[7]

The four psychotherapeutic postures described above are the only tools a therapist has. But they are powerful ones!

Parents often forget the degree of influence which an adult has on the mind of a child; far greater is that influence when the adult is also "a doctor" and has "an office," a special setting to which a child is brought (or, when an older adolescent, comes alone) for regular appointments during which they are granted the undivided attention of this person, a situation (being provided the sole attention of an adult) which they have probably not experienced since their earliest years. If the therapist knows how to interact helpfully with the child, the child will sense this and will want to come for treatment.

Choosing Your Child's Psychotherapist

The parents of one profoundly disturbed adolescent stated in amazement, after my first month of contact with her, that she didn't have to be reminded of her therapy appointments. "She really likes you," they said. My response was that although she might "like me," she came because she felt she was being healed. If she did not sense this, regardless of my "likability," she would not come.

An effective therapist is, simply, one who is capable —to the extent possible—of healing a child's emotional conflicts and ego deficiencies. This is done by providing for the child in each moment of their psychotherapy session the therapeutic posture that is most appropriate. This moment-to-moment interaction acts as a catalyst, causing the child to revise their erroneous theories about themselves and their environment, and facilitates the healing of their defective ego functions.

It is perhaps ironic that most of those psychologists and psychiatrists, and others with extensive training in healing disturbed children and adolescents, are least likely to work with them: often these clinicians treat only adults once they complete their training and begin their professional careers.

Some years ago I visited what is perhaps the most eminent psychoanalytic treatment and research setting in the United States. I still remember the disparaging tone used by an otherwise very friendly staff member as he said, "Oh, you work with the kiddies." Why are children (and particularly adolescents) so unpopular as patients?

I have often thought that before one works as a therapist with adults one should have had previous clinical training and experience with children. The great demand placed upon the therapist of a child for individualization of treatment, warmth and acceptance, honesty and compassion, is a superb experience for treating patients of all ages. One colleague of mine was treating an encopretic* six-year-old boy. A therapy session had just begun and the child, stating shyly that he had a present for his therapist, asked him to put out his hand. The therapist did and the child placed feces onto his palm. Such incidents are not extraordinary when one treats seriously disturbed young children. But the capacity to respond in a healing manner to these incidents is atypical. My colleague's response was not to express horror or discomfort: instead he thanked the boy for his gift and said he was very pleased that the child valued his visits with him.

* Encopresis is chronic fecal soiling. Alternating between periods of soiling and retention, these children may develop such serious physical difficulties that surgical intervention is required. Though it can derive from impairment of the nervous system or anatomical defect, this disorder results primarily from deep psychological conflict about growing up.

Such incidents are the least of the difficulties encountered when one works with children. Far more disdained by many psychologists and psychiatrists are the personality demands made upon them by children and adolescents: their demand to be treated in an individualized manner: to be "met" where they are at. Thus a therapist may be forced to play innumerable, excruciatingly boring games because these are what the child prefers. I recall with a feeling of horror my year of contact with a child whose favorite game was Chutes and Ladders, a board game of chance consisting of characters who would, in response to a roll of the dice, advance on the board, sometimes climbing the ladder (to reach the goal more quickly) and sometimes falling down the chute (thus reducing one's chance of winning).

The perception and honesty of young patients can also be jarring to the self-esteem of "a doctor." Adult patients may consider their therapist to be fat (or ugly, or dumb, or trying to conceal his loss of hair, and so on), but children (and especially adolescents) will *say* these things. A therapist who is unable to acknowledge as true unflattering assertions about themselves will have little success in healing young people.

Moreover, many adults have neither the desire nor the capacity to recall emotions which they first experienced as children. These feelings (as, being friendless in an uncaring world or being "putdown" by adults) are easily resurrected through contact with youth. I recall the rage I felt at the unhelpful manner in which an eight-year-old patient was being treated by his ill-equipped teacher, and when another (older) patient, experimenting with being self-assertive after a lifetime of physical and psychological abuse, was asked by a staff member of the vocational training program she was attending whether she had been in a mental hospital for "only two years."

Thus the treatment of children and adolescents has, almost by default, been left to less extensively trained individuals than psychologists and psychiatrists. Unfortunately, anyone can describe themselves as being "a therapist" since that title does not have any legal status with regard to education or training.

But even the degree of education and training implied by the title of "doctor" does not guarantee competence as a diagnostician and therapist. I have encountered more than a few ineffectual psychologists and psychiatrists, all with many years of experience. They had simply been doing the same wrong thing for many years.

If parents cannot rely solely upon the attributed qualifications of a psychotherapist, how can they determine when their child is being provided helpful and cost-effective treatment?

Characteristics of Effective Psychotherapy

1. WHEN YOUR CHILD'S THERAPY IS EFFECTIVE THEY WILL APPEAR BETTER!

I am amazed at those parents who accept vague reassurance as evidence of their child's effective treatment when they would never accept such vagaries with regard to the repair of their automobile or computer. Parents should never ask their child's therapist whether they are "getting better." They should be able to see such improvements for themselves. My response to all such questions is, "What changes have you noticed in your child?"

I once treated the almost incredibly disturbed very young daughter of a very troubled (and psychologically unsophisticated) physician. I responded with my question when he asked, after the child's initial two months of treatment, his question. He thought for several moments and then said, "She seems calmer." Some positive change should be evident after only several months of treatment, and may even appear after several weeks.

A child will get better in treatment if their treatment is effective! This is not to say that all emotional difficulties can be healed at a particular point in a child's life or, for that matter, that all difficulties can ever be healed. Some children and adolescents with severe ego deficiencies (a psychosis) or character disorders (a sociopathic personality) may, for all practical purposes, considering the immense treatment effort required, be incurable. These disturbances are the psychological equivalent of a fulminating cancer and their course may, because the damage occurred very early in the child's life, be irreversible. Parents consulting a psychotherapist willing to undertake treatment with these children should understand that progress will necessarily be slow.

But healing may be possible even for children whose disorders are most severe. A very gifted colleague was once consulted by the parents of a highly disturbed four-year-old boy. So disturbed was he that previous diagnostic studies had been unable to determine whether the child's difficulties reflected a psychological or neurological disorder or both combined in addition to mental retardation. My colleague saw this child for three diagnostic sessions; he too was unsure of the diagnosis. In the concluding moments of what was to be their last contact before the child was institutionalized in a long-term residential setting for retarded children, my friend turned away; the child, seeming to sense his despair, cried out, "If you want to help me you have to kill my mother!" My colleague began treating him. After several years of psychotherapy those symptoms which had been thought to reflect neurological damage (absent reflexes, an abnormal electroencephalogram record, and the like) disappeared. After further years of treatment the child's level of intelligence was found to be so high that it was virtually unmeasurable.

While cases of this kind are extraordinary, they do indicate that healing is possible even with the most severe psychological difficulties. However, this healing does demand a therapist who is well trained and experienced in treating such children. And such treatment is expensive: the child discussed above was treated daily on an outpatient basis for several years before less intensive treatment was possible. The cost of residential treatment in a good treatment facility (as compared with a custodial setting) may cost several hundred thousand dollars a year. But institutionalization (apart from brief periods, and these only for the most severe disorders) is rarely necessary: with most emotional difficulties some combination of individual psychotherapy, parent counseling, and (possibly) the provision of a special school setting will suffice to heal a child.

2. WHEN YOUR CHILD'S THERAPY IS EFFECTIVE YOU WILL FEEL BETTER!

Parents consult a therapist in time of crisis. They are frantic. Their desperation forces them to reveal to a stranger the most intimate details of their life. There are few more difficult burdens for parents to endure than those demands for care which a disturbed child presents. One important task for a therapist is to relieve them of this burden. Thus they should be available to them when needed. The responsibilities of an effective therapist go beyond the treatment session with the child: they must be prepared to take major responsibility for the child's life.

A child with a serious emotional difficulty is—psychologically—dying. And the stress which this imposes upon their parents causes *their* deterioration. My insistent statement to parents who tell me of their worry about their child is, "That's my business. You're paying me to worry about your child. You worry about your life!"

This assertion is not meant to indicate that I wish to intervene in or to take responsibility for all areas of a child's life (their clothing, the selection of a school for them, and so forth), but it emphasizes the fact that the parents' stress will diminish as the child becomes healed, and that the responsibility for this healing is mine. Thus the family's major worry has now become mine, although other practical concerns (financial difficulties, physical illness, and so on) remain theirs to resolve.

3. WHEN YOUR CHILD'S THERAPY IS EFFECTIVE YOU WILL UNDERSTAND YOUR CHILD BETTER!

Returning to Washington one winter evening, I was seated next to a woman in her early thirties. To while away the time, we shared some details of our lives. After learning that I was a psychologist, she spoke of her concern about her nine-year-old child. Because he had been doing poorly in school and seemed troubled she had taken him for weekly psychotherapy which had now lasted several years. The therapist had described the child's problems as reflecting a "developmental delay": one part of him was developing more slowly than another, thus causing his unhappiness and difficulties. But the mother was puzzled. Her child's behavior wasn't improving, and she didn't understand the therapist's explanation. Yet when she questioned him he merely repeated his "diagnosis."

I could well understand her dismay. The therapist's diagnosis was equally puzzling to me. If the child's difficulties reflected a "developmental delay," why then treat it for several years? Surely this problem would require no more than a brief counseling of the parents and child as to its cause and nature would alleviate the situation in time. Moreover, if the therapist's assessment was correct, why wasn't the child's behavior improving?

This mother's situation is not unusual. Often, parents are not given an adequate explanation of the nature of their child's difficulty. This explanation need not be one in which technical terms are used, but it should be so clear and comprehensive that the parents have no further questions about the nature of the child's difficulty or the process of treatment.

Parents should never feel uncomfortable when, because they do not understand some aspect of their child's behavior, they consult the therapist. Parents are paying for service: they have the right to understand what they're paying for! It is the obligation of the therapist to provide this understanding. If they don't or can't, then find another therapist for your child!

Because the behavior of severely troubled children can be puzzling (and often terrifying) to parents who must not only live with this situation but cope with all of the other practical difficulties the family confronts, I often suggest that both parents meet with me on a once monthly basis to discuss their concerns, to increase their comfort. Not infrequently I provide a parent individual treatment sessions where my primary focus is not the child's life but the parent's.

I insist that all patients telephone me whenever they feel the need, making clear that I am never angry when telephoned by a patient in such circumstances, but am disappointed when they hesitate to do so. My receptiveness to out-of-session contact has almost never been abused. I rarely receive emergency telephone calls when no emergency (as perceived by the patient) exists. Actually this policy also redounds to my benefit: I would prefer to deal over the telephone with those minor crises which can erupt in the course of treatment than be faced with the necessity of confronting the major psychological emergency which would more likely develop were these smaller symptoms of distress ignored.

Honest Answers You Thought You'd Never Receive to Some Intimate Questions About Psychotherapy You Thought You'd Never Dare Ask

1. How is it possible for a therapist's contact with my child to change their life when their parents' virtually twenty-four-hour daily contact with them doesn't?

If the period a child spends in their therapist's office was all the contact there is, little change would occur. But this is not the case. A therapist's contact with their patient continues even when the two are apart!

Some years ago I was treating an eight-year-old boy once weekly for a period of about a year. Then, because of my planned move to another part of the country, arrangements were made to transfer him to another therapist. Six weeks before my departure I informed the boy of this prospective change. He said nothing but the following week he brought in a drawing. It depicted my departure from the city in an airplane. Under the drawing he had written, "I know you have to go. But I'm sorry you're going."

I felt very moved. I wanted to hug him and to tell him that I would miss him too, but I could not. It would not be helpful to him. It was healthy that he mourn my departure and healthy that he be angry, an emotion he would (hopefully) work out to some degree in our remaining weeks of contact and resolve completely with his next therapist. We had worked together on his difficulties for a year and significant improvement occurred. Now our involvement with each other was coming to an end. So I told him, "When two people have been together for as long as we have and have shared as many experiences as we have, then each person has built up an image, a picture, of the other person in their mind, a picture they will have all their life. So any time that you want us to be together all you need do is to close your eyes and think of me, and then we'll be together again." Johnny closed his eyes and turned his face away from mine and cried out in wonder, "I see you!" Then he opened his eyes, faced another part of my office, and said, "I see you now, too!"

Psychotherapy "works" because the child (or adolescent or adult) creates an image of the therapist in their mind, an image which they invest with significant power. It is this image which provides a continual healing influence on the child's mind even when they are at home, alone, or asleep.

But this phenomenon is surely not difficult to understand. Most people have had contact in their lives with an older, trusted person (perhaps a teacher or a neighbor) whose influence had far greater effect on them than the brevity of the contact would otherwise indicate.

2. *Do people become therapists because of their own personal problems?*

Yes. Or at least most do. The vocational choice of most psychologists and psychiatrists derives, at least initially, and unconsciously, from their own personal problems— and there is nothing wrong with that. What is wrong is when, having completed their training and entering the profession, a therapist still holds the erroneous belief that becoming a doctor will, in and of itself, provide them with a feeling of security or help them to achieve emotional fulfillment.*

*An article by Richard D. Chessick, M.D., Ph.D., in the January 1978 issue of the *Bulletin of the Menninger Clinic* ("The Sad Soul of the Psychiatrist") discusses this quite movingly.

Being a therapist does not mean that a person has resolved all of their own emotional conflicts: no one ever does. But a patient does have a right to expect that a therapist is so aware of their conflicts that these will not interfere in their work.   Each therapist works best with patients who have a particular kind of difficulty. Gradually, as they gain experience, the categories of emotional difficulty with which they can work effectively will increase. But they will never cover the full range of human problems! When a therapist feels uncomfortable working with a particular patient, they have one of three alternatives: to analyze, alone, the cause of their discomfort and thus eliminate it; to share their difficulty with a colleague and gain help for it; or to discharge the patient to another therapist. Those clinicians claiming to be gifted in their treatment of all patients are, almost certainly, effective with few; but they never discover this because they are generally reluctant to submit their work to the scrutiny of their peers.

3. Why does therapy take so long?

It doesn't. Or at least the initial improvement should soon be evident. This improvement can be particularly rapid with young children, even those whose emotional disorders are most severe. Some improvement in the child (increased control over their behavior, improved performance in school, and so on) should appear within, at the most, three to six months of treatment, although the permanent remedying of their conflicts and the healing of their ego limitations (if they exist) will take longer. How much longer will depend upon the severity of the difficulty and the degree of progress the child is capable of making.

Some children (particularly adolescents) cannot immediately deal with certain difficulties: they must be older, must have gained a greater sense of who they are before they can risk revealing more of themselves to another person. A colleague once treated a severely disturbed seventeen-year-old girl for about eight months.

During this period the girl made some progress in ordering her life. She then discontinued treatment, stating that she would return when her life was more settled. Six years later the girl telephoned, asking to return to treatment. She could now contemplate changes which had seemed intolerable years before.

There is no fixed length of time for psychotherapy. Its duration depends on the evaluation of the therapist as to whether further healing is possible. This evaluation must be continual, since the patient changes with their experience of each life situation and with each psychotherapy session.

Yet, psychotherapy is a slow process. Its length of time depends upon the severity of the difficulty present when the child is brought for treatment. The existence of a symptom indicates that a difficulty has already existed for a considerable period during which time it has interfered with the development of the child's mind. The longer the symptom has persisted, and the greater the effect upon their functioning, the more difficult is the task of the therapist. Ideally there would exist so adequate and comprehensive a network of parent education and child evaluation and psychotherapy services that difficulties would always be alleviated before they reached major proportions.

The effectiveness of psychotherapy (and therefore the speed of improvement) also reflects the ability of the therapist to provide the correct psychotherapeutic posture (or combination of postures) at each moment of their interaction with the patient.

4. What if my child doesn't want to see a therapist even though I feel they need professional help?

Children (and adults) often have an inaccurate concept of what a therapist does. Perceiving them as being one who will offer criticism or advice (what has already been provided, without apparent usefulness, by relatives and friends), they see little reason to endure yet another well-meaning person. They sense the terrors that lurk within their mind and fear to face those discomforting thoughts and feelings which would upset their precarious mental stability were they to visit "a doctor," one who might demand that they describe these experiences they so fear to speak of.

A child (or adolescent) will be more willing to consult a therapist if the situation is explained to them properly by their parents: "We're concerned about your life. We feel you're unhappy but are unable to help you and would like you to come with us to consult a professional person, one who can work with you to achieve those goals in your life that you want." While a child will (most usually) be accompanied by their parents at the initial consultation, an older adolescent may prefer to travel there unaccompanied.

What should a parent do if their child (or adolescent) still refuses to seek treatment? Insist on it! Don't be intimidated by your child's angry threats (that, for example, they will refuse to speak to the doctor). Once they are in the therapist's office, you've done your job! Now it's up to the therapist to interact with your child so that they will want to return or to advise you so that if the child doesn't want to return you will understand their difficulties and feel more comfortable in coping with them.

Therapy isn't always the answer to a troubled child's difficulties, but understanding *always* alleviates the situation they present in the family.

5. *Can a therapist "read a child's mind"?*

They must be able to if they are to help your child. The way that a therapist diagnoses the nature of a child's difficulties is by analyzing their speech and behavior using the tools granted them by their academic knowledge of human development and psychopathology and by their clinical experience. It is the insight verbalized by the therapist which gives a child the feeling that their therapist can "read my mind."

6. *Isn't therapy too expensive?*

It depends on how you look at it. Some years ago a divorced neighbor consulted me about her seventeen-year-old son. The boy, although very bright, was doing poorly in school and recently had begun speaking of suicide. Would I see the boy? I said that I would. I received a call that night about 9:00 P.M. Her son had arrived, was furious that I had been consulted, but would be over to speak with me in a few minutes. I spoke first alone with the boy, then with his mother, then with the two of them together. I treated the boy once weekly, in individual psychotherapy, for about six months. At the end of that period the boy was doing well in school, had a girl friend, and was working at a part-time job. He then decided to terminate treatment. I agreed, feeling that although serious difficulties still existed, he could not tolerate further therapy at that point in his life. The total cost of the boy's treatment was under $3,000. Had he been hospitalized for only one week (as was a serious possibility considering the severity of his difficulties) the cost would have been greater. I don't consider the fee exorbitant (or even high), considering the changes that were accomplished.

Yet I do recognize that meeting the cost of psychotherapy can be difficult for a family (or an individual): removing $100 (or more) from any family's weekly net income is a significant deduction (although most families have some form of health insurance providing substantial reimbursement and many states offer excellent low-cost insurance coverage). But, unfortunately, there is no alternative. Severe psychological disorders are analogous to severe physical pathology: the cost for the care and treatment are comparable. The more effective the therapist, the more rapid the progress and the lower the cost.

7. *What about "organicity"? Aren't children "born with" difficulties?*

There are few more misunderstood terms than *organicity* or *organic involvement*. All people are biological organisms. Each is born with a particular capacity to tolerate certain kinds of stress and to develop defenses against it. When one speaks of organicity in emotional disturbance one is asserting that a child was born with a limited capacity to develop defenses against a particular kind of stress they experienced early in their life, or now has a biologically limited capacity to heal the mental damage which occurred because they experienced this intolerable stress. An emotional difficulty (a neurosis, psychosis, character disorder, psychophysiological disorder) is the joint product of a child's biologically based capacity to develop healthfully using their existing defenses against stress and an environmental stress. Not one or the other.

Even mental retardation may be partly the product of emotional difficulties or childhood experiences which don't facilitate the development of a child's intellectual capacities. A child's inherited biological structure does not determine their personality or level of intelligence: it sets those limits within which, through experience with the environment, their intellectual capacities and personality structures become formed.

To describe a situation as reflecting "organicity" is not to explain it: these words merely demand that the required explanation be even more comprehensive.

8. *But isn't "hyperactivity" organic in nature?*

An investigator classified into five categories the major types of research studies used to investigate the possibility of organic involvement in the hyperactive behavior of children: the study of the electrical activity of the brain, the study of neurological soft signs (e.g., immature reflexes), studies hypothesizing a biochemical imbalance in the nervous system, studies of pregnancy and birth complications, and genetic studies hypothesizing deviant chromosomal structure. His conclusion, based upon an exhaustive survey of the research literature, is that there is virtually no factual evidence to support the hypothesis that hyperactivity in children derives from organic factors.[8,9]

But don't children's learning disabilities result primarily from biological causes?

I can do no better than quote the following: " . . . when a child's problems with reading become the disease of dyslexia, many parents, educators, and "scientists" somehow feel a greater sense of hope. "Can't-read-itis" might do as well, but dyslexia has a more scientific ring to it, as does dyscalculia instead of "trouble-with-math." . . . The archetype is, of course, minimal brain dysfunction (MBD), the paradigm of mythological diseases in children. Beginning often with real behaviors and real problems (although the involvement of family or school is often underplayed), researchers, pediatricians, child therapists, teachers, and parents have all persuaded each other that something is amiss in the child's brain. The research supporting such a belief is not only abominable from a scientific point of view, but is often contaminated by drug company money. One is reminded of drapetomania (Drapetes—a runaway slave in Greek mythology), a disease of Negro slaves, characterized by a mania for running away. It was first diagnosed and reported (1851) by Dr. Samuel Cartwright in the New Orleans Medical and Surgical Journal, but virtually disappeared after the Emancipation Proclamation.

"Learning disability (LD) is another newly discovered brain disease. If not detected early, when it manifests itself in the school setting, it progresses to gross motor impairment; i.e., juvenile delinquency. As with MBD, LD is diagnosed by inference, analogy, and circularity; the behaviors are considered the symptoms of a disease, which in turn is characterized by the behaviors. The search for a neurophysiological basis is as strained as it is self-serving, but virtually an entire psychoeducational industry has nonetheless grown up around the crude theories".[9]

10. *Instead of treating a child individually, why not see them as a member of a group of children, thereby treating many children simultaneously? Wouldn't this be more economical and equally effective?*

The essence of individual psychotherapeutic treatment is that a patient can be provided—on a moment-to-moment basis—with that therapeutic posture which is most helpful to their healing. This cannot be done when one is interacting with many children simultaneously. While group therapy can be useful to certain children with certain types of difficulties, it is not a substitute for individual psychotherapy; nor is the meeting of the therapist with the child and their whole family (family therapy). While I almost always have regular contact with the parents of those children I treat, I have not found meeting as a family to be useful, and certainly not the treatment of choice, except when a child's emotional disturbance is reactive, that is, the product of a specific, short-lived family difficulty.

11. *Wouldn't treating emotionally disturbed children with drugs be more economical?*

A drug is a chemical which, by interacting with other chemicals, alters the body's biochemical environment, thus modifying its functioning. Through this modification changes occur in the individual's emotions and perception, these changes being reflected in their interaction with the environment.

Drugs cannot heal a child's mind such that it reaches a higher level of development, which is the purpose of psychotherapy, but they are occasionally helpful in the treatment of children's emotional disturbances. For example, the level of anxiety experienced by the more severely disturbed (particularly hospitalized) adolescents can be very great: it is only humane to provide them with temporary medication to alleviate their suffering. I hold no belief that people should suffer unnecessarily.

12. *How does a therapist relate to a child at their first meeting?*

By keeping in mind that they are first a human being, by responding as one person to another. But also by remembering that they are a scientist and a healer, one who is trained to understand the mind and to heal its disorders. The therapist tries to provide an atmosphere in which the child feels so comfortable that they are able to communicate their most intimate and troubling thoughts and feelings. The therapist realizes that the child may be suffering greatly and tries not to increase that suffering. Thus if the child is unable to speak or is hostile, the therapist's attitude is not one of condemnation or disdain but rather reflects their knowledge that the child may have little choice in their behavior. By their attitude the therapist tries to communicate the following:

"I realize that you may be in pain and suffering greatly. I do not wish to increase your suffering. Because I do not know you well, some of my questions, inevitably, will hurt. But my purpose is not to hurt you but to learn about you so that we can work together to alleviate your suffering.

"We are entering onto a long dark road. Our journey may be difficult and there may be some pain, but I will be with you all of the way. And at the end of our journey you will be healed."

13. *It sounds like there is an element of love in psychotherapy.*

Yes, there is.

14. But what is psychotherapy really like?
Read on.

Notes

1. Sigmund Freud, *Introductory Lectures on Psycho-Analysis.* Standard Edition of the Complete Psychological Works of Sigmund Freud, ed. and trans. James Strachey, Vol. 16 (London: The Hogarth Press, Ltd, 1917).

2. Heinrich Racker, *Transference and Countertransference* (New York: International Universities Press, Inc., 1968), p. 34-35.

3. "Transactions of the Topeka Psychoanalytic Society," *Bulletin of the Menninger Clinic* 41 (1977): 595-598.

4. Alan Stone, *Mental Health and Law* (New York: Aronson, 1976), p.252.

5. G. Simpson, "CNS Effects of Neuroleptic Agents," *Psychiatric Annals* 5 (1975), 53-60.

6. *Pharmacy Times*, March 1974.

7. David Marholin II, and David Phillips, "Methodological Issues in Psychopharmacological Research: Chlorpromazine—A Case in Point," *American Journal of Orthopsychiatry* 46 (1976): 477-495-

8. Dennis R. Dubey, "Organic Factors in Hyperkinesis: A Critical Evaluation," *American Journal of Orthopsychiatry* 46 (1976): 353-366.

9. Lee Coleman, "Problem Kids and Preventive Medicine: The Making of an Odd Couple," *American Journal of Orthopsychiatry* 48 (1978): 56-70.

PART TWO

Of Children and Their Doctors at The Hospital

Introduction to Part II

My years of working at The Hospital changed both my patients and me. Because psychotherapy consists of a special type of relationship, the therapist themselves cannot be unchanged by their work. Usually these changes are beneficial: from their experience they learn more about human conflict and becomes a more effective healer. But occasionally the personal difficulties of the therapist are so great that, when they encounter the extraordinary stress that results from treating severely disturbed patients, tragedy results. "Jim's" death, described in Chapter 9, was one of these tragedies.*

*A paper by Gordon Bermark, published in a volume of the *American Journal of Psychoanalysis* (1977. pp. 141-146), has itemized some of these stresses: the emotional drain of being constantly empathic; the long delay in achieving results in the treatment of patients; the provocation to suicide caused by seeing suicide in patients; the need for the therapist to control their emotion; and the separation anxiety aroused when a patient whom one has treated for many years leaves treatment.

I arrived at The Hospital believing in the capacity of psychoanalytically oriented psychotherapy to heal even the most severe psychological disorders, such as those of Robert and John, who are discussed in the following chapters. My experience with them and many later patients confirmed this belief. The road we traveled was long and difficult but the goals which we achieved were worthy of the journey. Yet only after I left The Hospital, having realized both the power and the limitations of this method of treatment, did I come to recognize the importance of hope and faith and love to the healing process.

CHAPTER SEVEN

Robert: The Gentle, Frightened Jewish Boy Who Believed in Jesus and Beat the Devil

I recall very clearly those years with Robert when we stood alone against the madness which enveloped him, against a world which scorned him, against some at The Hospital who could not understand him and who, like so many in his life, believed him to be incurable.

My thoughts of those years are not of a hospital building, or of my office with its view of the river, or of the foliage which in autumn caused the winding country roads to blaze with color. Instead I think of Robert, of gentle lonely Robert, and, of course, of Mr. Giraffe, warm, accepting Mr. Giraffe who awaited us in the clearing at the bend in the road.

In the initial pages of Chapter 2 I described Robert's early life: his childhood, isolated and barren of intimacy; his diagnosis as "incurable"; his years of wandering through a small Baptist church in his southern town; his admission, at fourteen years of age, to The Hospital.

I described his early months of treatment: his test of my honesty; his unsuccessful suicide attempt; his growing need for contact with me; and how we came to engage in those unconventional but therapeutic games which played so significant a role in his healing. I now continue my description of those early days in our relationship, of those days before Mr. Giraffe entered our lives, and before Robert beat the Devil.

It was through our relationship that Robert became less lonely, that he first allowed himself to experience warmth and to express love. His relationship, that is, with both me and Mr. Giraffe, of course.

Robert had other relationships at The Hospital: with Nina, the voluptuous, seventeen-year-old pornographic film star who taught him about sexuality; and Arnold, the incredibly damaged youth with whom he so strongly identified; and . . . But I am getting ahead of my story, or Robert's story, or that of Mr. Giraffe.

In those years we were together Robert allowed himself to trust me and, through trusting me, he discovered his own nature and opened himself to life. Robert used to say that only by believing in Jesus could his life be changed. Certainly this belief kept him from suicide in his moments of most profound despair and helped him to beat the Devil. But, again, I am getting ahead of my story.

No hospital can ever be a desirable place to live. Even the smallest institution, in order to function, must impose on its inhabitants rules which govern their lives and assign people with whom they must live. Arnold was Robert's first roommate. The two shared a room containing two pieces each of identical furniture: a bed with a fluorescent light above it, a chest of drawers, a study desk, lamp, and chair.

Robert's bookshelf held a Bible and several books about clocks and electric motors. Arnold's bookshelf was empty, like his life. This emptiness may be the reason why I never knew very much about Arnold despite our innumerable, though casual, contacts. Or my lack of knowledge may reflect the fact that he left The Hospital during my first year there. Or perhaps it is because Robert first spoke of him only some years later. But by then it was too late to learn more about Arnold: he was a patient at a large state hospital, relinquished to the world of his own madness, forgotten by all at The Hospital except Robert.

Arnold was a tall, profoundly disturbed adolescent. Barely toilet trained, unkempt, and with a voracious appetite, he seemed an unlikely friend indeed for the extremely well-mannered and gentle youth who was his roommate. But they did care for each other. Robert sensed that Arnold would not harm him despite his threats, and Arnold never did.

When I first learned of these threats several years later, I was then so aware of Robert's secretiveness that I didn't ask why he hadn't sought my aid. Instead I simply said, "You really suffered in those years." And he had.

During Robert's first several years at The Hospital he spent little time in school, those small classes in which adolescent patients participated. When he did, it was not to learn mathematics or history but to dance quietly in the back of the classroom. Although he didn't make much noise, Robert's overt craziness so disturbed the other patients that I rarely received complaints from his teachers when he frequently missed classes. Or perhaps their lack of concern reflected their knowledge of his whereabouts: during much of the school day, while the other students attended classes, he lay on a bench outside my office.

What was this "craziness" which schoolteachers and patients alike found so disturbing? For Robert was considered different even by many patients at The Hospital.

Many childhood experiences—learning to use one's body, experiencing and expressing feelings, being self-assertive, enjoying warmth and closeness—were unknown to Robert. Only now, at adolescence, did he begin to commit himself to life, to give way to the forces of his nature. Much like a young child who, by imagining himself in play as a jet pilot, nurtures those seeds which years later mature into his commitment to a vocation, so too did Robert in those early years, through our games* and within our relationship, experiment with those feelings and experiences out of which mature behavior and capacities arise.

One day piercing screams leapt through the corridors. Several patients covered their ears and ran shrieking down the hall. Fists pounded on my locked** office door, then cries: "What's going on in there?" "It's Robert," I called out. "Oh," was the response, then the sound of their footsteps echoed down the corridor on the hard wooden floor.

During this earliest of our games, our dramatic re-enactment—with changes—of events in Robert's life, I portrayed a hospital attendant who often harassed Robert (and me) about his eating habits. "Can't we do something about his eating?"he would storm at me. "Look at him," and I did. Robert was a handsome boy, slightly overweight, but growing rapidly.

* The origin of these games is described in Chapter 2.
** Because many patients at The Hospital had only fragile control over their behavior, they often opened doors and walked into rooms uninvited. To forestall interruption the door of my office was always locked during a patient's therapy session. At other times it was almost always open. In this way I became friendly with virtually all of the patients at The Hospital, many of whom would, informally, "drop in."

I repeatedly explained to the attendant that eating was one of the few comforting experiences in Robert's life. That, as his conflicts were resolved and he discovered other satisfactions, he would naturally eat less than the two to three portions he now demanded at each meal. When he was ready to lose weight he would.

But my explanations to the attendant and his lack of success in changing my attitude, did not dissuade him from trying to change Robert's eating habits. Even years later he would look suspiciously when Robert, now five inches taller and forty-five pounds lighter, requested more fried chicken. Fried chicken. I well remember those days in which it played so extensive a role in my conversations with this man and, more understandably, in my game with Robert.

In this game Robert was punched by the attendant (portrayed by me) when, despite repeated admonitions, he still demanded more calorie-laden food. While my punches were, of course, feigned, few, hearing Robert's shrieks, would have thought so. So loud and shrill were his cries that, after several weeks, I asked that they be moderated lest the functioning of the institution (and my hearing) become impaired.

Another game we played during these months derived from Robert's school experience before coming to The Hospital. For most of his life Robert had attended a school for emotionally disturbed children near his home. The school had a behavior modification orientation, a student being provided pleasures (as, going on school trips or being provided snacks) only after he had earned a sufficient number of stars (by his good behavior) to purchase them. Because of Robert's profound emotional difficulties, his "earnings" were often inadequate for the available "purchases." Thus the school's procedures only increased the frustration in this very troubled child's life.

My role in this game was that of Mrs. Ross, a teacher who Robert hated for her inability to understand that he was unable to behave as she demanded. Over the course of many weeks of playing this game with me, Robert so changed that his response to "her" statement, "You can't have noooo snack cause you don't have enough stars," went from spitting at her to punching her to curses ("you're a fucking bitch, Mrs. Ross!"). The changes in Robert's mode of expressing anger approximated the sequence that occurs in normal development, but far more quickly.

For several years these games made up most of our interaction. I enjoyed playing many of them. They appealed to those childlike elements in my own personality which I had revealed to few people in my life. But some of the games we played were excruciatingly repetitious.

During one of these games I portrayed a department store owner, Mr. Briggs, who sold Robert whatever clock he wanted. For months our conversation consisted of my being asked whether the "store" sold a particular clock, my reaching for the (imaginary) clock, "wrapping it," and handing it to Robert. Because of his extraordinary knowledge of and my virtually total ignorance of antique and modern clocks, I was required to learn, under his tutelage, their most arcane characteristics. My error, or any attempt to alter the wording of the dialogue between Robert and "Mr. Briggs," would result in Robert's demand that we begin the game anew.

Robert's experimenting with feelings and behavior, his allowing himself to act assertively and to express anger openly, did not occur only in my office. It was early one summer afternoon when Robert came—unscheduled—to my office and said, "I threw shit at Pat."* He then asked whether I felt his behavior was "good" or "bad."

*Pat was an attendant on Robert's ward.

I said that I was proud of him, that I knew how difficult it was for him to assert himself, particularly with such courage. Robert beamed and shook my hand vigorously. A few minutes later I apologized to Pat for Robert's behavior and expressed my gratitude that he had been able to accept it. I said that such acceptance was crucial to Robert's healing: in time he would express himself more maturely, verbally rather than physically.

Pat downplayed the discomfort he had experienced. "I just changed my clothes," he said. But he questioned whether Robert was, in fact, improving, for some of his behavior was very peculiar. Like his showering. Robert would spend hours under the shower, reveling in the experience of warm water flowing over his body. I tried, without success, to explain that Robert was attempting, symbolically through his showering, to provide himself with the warmth he had lacked as a child. But Pat could not understand. Although he was an excellent attendant, Pat lacked the ability, as Robert had said, "to understand that what's important is what's going on inside a person."

In time, Robert was allowed to leave the hospital grounds for brief periods. While his initial excursions were limited to walking to a local diner for a hamburger, he soon began attending services at a local Presbyterian church in the company of three other patients. Probably few churches in America can boast worshipers as varied as these. One boy was Catholic, two (including Robert) were Jewish, and one was actually Presbyterian.

Walking to church along the winding country road each Sunday morning, two in front and two behind, they presented an unremarkable appearance. Yet, Calvin, thirteen years old, had been hospitalized after trying to smother to death his four-year-old sister. He spoke of little except the dangers of the world and his desire to return to his home in a far-off state.

David, a fifteen-year-old Chinese-American boy, had one of the highest IQs among the patient population. He had been misdiagnosed as being "learning disabled" at an early age and been receiving inappropriate treatment until his admission to The Hospital. Profoundly depressed and appearing far older than his years, he had once gone to the office of a local attorney and asked to draw up a will. The attorney had narrowly missed falling from his chair when, in response to his query as to the marital status of the gentleman facing him, he was informed, "Married? Are you off your bird? I'm only fifteen!"

Henry, sixteen years old, was so emotionally constricted that he was virtually unable to speak. In defense against his great, unexpressed feelings of rage, his face held an almost continuous smile.

Fortunate is the pastor whose congregation contains such devoted members. They attended early morning service and remained for the coffee hour; they attended late morning service and remained for the social hour. Sunday afternoon found them still at church, attending the Bible study class. They sang more loudly, prayed more fervently, and attended church more regularly than any of the other parishioners. They helped the pastor open the church in the morning and were with him as he locked the doors in the evening, often accompanying him home and seeking an invitation to dinner. The pastor's patience was remarkable.

Robert believed in Jesus. Only by believing in His divinity, he felt, could he be "saved" and come to have a life filled with love and warmth. It was probably this belief that kept him from attempting suicide until that fateful day (described in Chapter 2) when he drank what he believed to be his "last cup of water," touched the high voltage cable, and, contrary to his expectations, was unharmed.

I do not doubt that it was Robert's belief that death through suicide would preclude his entrance into the "Kingdom of the Lord" kept this horribly suffering boy from later seeking that peace through death which he so yearned for.

And in those terrible days which have yet to be described, when his suffering was so great and his grasp on life so precarious that he was never allowed to walk unaccompanied for fear that he would, in a moment of anguish, destroy himself, it was partially Robert's religious commitment, his conviction that he did not have *the right* to take his own life, which kept him alive. That, and his unquestioning trust in me and the comfort he derived from Mr. Giraffe. But these events lay far in the future. Robert's goals over the next several years were ordinary ones: to understand girls, and to achieve intimacy.

Robert had never experienced intimacy. Fearing human contact, he had rarely allowed himself to be touched by another person or to accept warmth. It was at The Hospital that he first opened himself to these fundamental human needs.

Few staff members failed to sense the difference between Robert and the other patients: his gentleness and courtesy, even in his moments of greatest suffering, accorded him a respect which (unfortunately) was not always granted to patients. Equally striking was the appearance he presented to others, as being one who was apart from people. Like many whose lives lack early fundamental experiences, Robert seemed to be existing apart from rather than with people, as if he had never gained entrance, by passage through an adequately nurturing early life experience, into the body of humanity. Perhaps this was why, in my years of treating Robert, I often felt like holding him in my arms, nurturing him as one would a very young child.

While I did not provide him with more than symbolic approximations of the physical nurturing he had never allowed himself to experience (for this would have been incompatible with my role as his therapist), others did. An elderly, very maternal nurse, Irma, would often, in response to his invitation, hug and kiss him. And I can still visualize this teenage boy running down the corridor into her arms.

Early in our relationship Robert was unable to assert himself at all: he could not even tell me when he preferred not to discuss a topic which I had raised. At these times he would say, "Please get me a cup of milk." My leaving the office to comply with his request forestalled the conversation he wished to avoid. His request also, by causing me to furnish him food, provided him with the symbolic equivalent of a nurturing experience he had lacked as a child.

Thus Robert finally gained the nurturing he required, physically from Irma and psychologically through his twice-daily psychotherapy sessions with me.

A psychotherapist, much like a parent, often perceives small changes in a child but remains unaware of those larger changes seen by strangers. So it was with Robert. When I began treating him, his ability to communicate directly was so limited that I rarely asked him a question. Robert was so guarded and inexperienced in verbalizing his feelings that he could not express even an ordinary emotion as, for example, "I felt hurt when Pat criticized me." Thus his ability and desire to communicate, using such statements as had described Pat, his attendant, reflected a great advance in his psychological development.

While I was aware of the changes in his mind indicated by his asking a particular question, or discussing a previously avoided topic, or responding to me differently (such as allowing himself to express anger, if only covertly), it was others who first noticed the broader changes in his behavior.

An attendant reported the fury which Robert had expressed when he couldn't find his bathing suit and thus, unavoidably, missed swimming one day. He grabbed the attendant by the shoulder and raged at him, "It's your job to get me a bathing suit. Now you get the car and buy me one!" Shortly thereafter several windows were broken, a common occurrence at The Hospital. But surprise among the patients was augmented by happy smiles among the staff when the perpetrator became known: gentle and (formerly) unaggressive Robert.

Now, having become increasingly verbal and assertive, Robert embarked on the next step in his development: learning about girls.

Will I ever forget Nina? Appearing far older than her years when she was first admitted to The Hospital at the age of sixteen, she had already starred in several well-known pornographic movies. A stranger who viewed them together, handsome Robert and lovely Nina, might imagine them to be an ideal teenage couple. But relating to Nina proved a great burden for Robert. She would behave seductively toward him but, when he drew close, run away. Finally, she rejected him and favored another boy with her attention. Robert was disconsolate in the weeks following the break-up of his "affair." But he found consolation in an unexpected source, for it was during those days of sorrow following Robert's failure in his first attempt to achieve intimacy with a peer that Mr. Giraffe entered our lives.

I no longer recall how it happened yet from those days onward, a very tall, very gentle, very understanding, most handsome, quite silent, and wholly imaginary giraffe began accompanying us as we walked along the heavily wooded country roads near The Hospital. Thereafter as we left the grounds each day, we greeted him where he awaited us: in the clearing at the bend in the road.

Most often Mr. Giraffe supported us merely by being with us as we traveled those isolated roads, speaking of Robert's troubling thoughts and feelings. But at times he played a greater role in Robert's treatment. One of Robert's most fervent interests during this period was of "husbands and wives sleeping together." Now, before we parted at the end of our hourly contact, Robert would often ask Mr. Giraffe whether he would be sleeping with Mrs. Giraffe that night.

It was on one of those afternoons, as we three walked down the road following his demand that Mr. Giraffe beat up a thoughtless attendant, that Robert hesitantly said to me, "I love you." I didn't answer. I stood there thinking, on that silent road. Did I too love him? My commitment to his healing had been very great: no child in the history of The Hospital except Eva (whom we will meet in Chapter 9) had been treated on such an intensive basis as Robert. My years of contact with Robert had caused me to regard him almost as my child. I remembered the day an attendant asked, "Who does Robert resemble? His mother or his father? He's such a handsome boy," and my response, "Neither. He looks like his therapist." We laughed for we were both aware that my commitment to Robert's healing was greater than was perhaps wise, and that I was aware of this.

And so I said nothing to Robert that day because, indeed, there was nothing I could say. Did I love him? If the word conveys commitment to his healing and the willingness to be present at any moment he needed me, then surely I did. But my love was a special kind of love for despite my commitment I was always aware that Robert was my patient and not my child. My task was to heal him, not to parent him or to love him though for psychotherapy to be effective it must contain elements of both. Were I to allow myself to act only as his parent, his further healing through our relationship would inevitably cease. And he would grow to hate me, sensing that I had failed him, and I would come to despise myself.

And so Robert and I and Mr. Giraffe walked back down the road toward The Hospital, and Robert's psychological growth continued.

It was in those days after Mr. Giraffe entered our lives that we began to play that game which, of all our games, we most enjoyed: Robert's victory over the Devil. Traveling by train to the depths of Hell (which lay, in our game, under Washington's Union Station), Robert met the

Devil (as portrayed by his therapist), who described to him the living conditions in that nether region: eternal abominable food and excruciating work. Finding that his pleading for permission to leave merely increased the resolve of the Devil to detain him, Robert battled him and, after a furious (feigned) struggle, trounced him, only then achieving permission to re-board the train back to earth. This game, too, we played innumerable times.

Meanwhile, other changes were occurring in Robert's life. He now spent his time in school working on his academic studies rather than dancing, and he began playing the guitar, this being a popular pastime at The Hospital.

The change in Robert over the next few years was very great. We rarely, any longer, played "our games," and Mr. Giraffe gradually receded from our lives. Our discussions during his therapy sessions now concerned his fears of independence and self-assertion, and thoughts about his educational and vocational future after he left The Hospital. And he wanted to return to his family which lived a thousand miles from The Hospital.

Robert had been at The Hospital longer than most patients and, seeing his friends leave, he wanted to follow their example. But he was not yet ready to return home or to live independently in the community. He chose instead to live in The Residence, a halfway house located in a small city about twenty-five miles from The Hospital. The patients there had more freedom (as, not having a curfew) and responsibility (sharing shopping and cooking chores) than those living at The Hospital. They also had a greater opportunity for participation in community activities there than at the geographically isolated Hospital.

In the morning, the patients at The Residence helped to prepare breakfast and performed their assigned cleaning chores; the rest of the day they spent in school at The Hospital, after which they returned to The Residence for their evening meal. It was in those evenings, with a courage which few teenagers could match, that Robert began to socialize, extensively and unprotected, for the first time in his life. He went to a pizza shop and thrust himself into conversations with the local high school youth. So great was his initial success with the girls that he was once warned by a jealous boy to keep away or he would be beaten up. Robert, realizing that the boy was not serious, continued his social adventures. But I learned of these threats only some months later, after Robert had returned to The Hospital, dejected and broken in spirit.

Leaving The Hospital had been difficult for him. It had been his home for many years. He had, among the staff and patients, created an intensely supportive and available family presence which nurtured him when he felt in need. But, more importantly, upon leaving The Hospital even to enter the almost equally supportive Residence, Robert came to realize for the first time in his life just how crippling his conflicts were. He threw himself into the world and, although achieving some success, was shattered by his inability to gratify his overwhelming need for intimacy and his desire to be socially and economically self-sufficient in the larger world of which he was a part but from which he had been, thus far, shielded.

Over the ensuing months Robert became increasingly nervous and less able to meet even those minimal requirements for independent activity demanded by the staff at The Residence. And so Robert returned to The Hospital and immediately grew calm, for he had returned to the only place in the world where he could not be rejected and where no demand beyond his ability would ever be placed upon him. He returned to The Hospital, to Irma's arms and caresses, to "our games," to the glasses of milk which had been absent from his life for so long, and, again, to the comforting presence of Mr. Giraffe, who now re-entered our lives.

Now being profoundly depressed and suicidal, Robert spoke only of his belief in Jesus, of his certainty that he was "saved" and would someday achieve "a life filled with everlasting love and warmth." It was partially this conviction that kept him alive in those fearful days when his mind teemed with thoughts of self-destruction.

After many months Robert was once again able to speak of his feelings, his fears of intimacy and self-assertion, and his future. It was then that he discovered the origin of a puzzling desire he had expressed since earliest childhood: his need "to go east." It derived from that period when, consumed by terrifying nightmares, he had sought comfort in his parents' room. The window in their room faced east.

Finally, Robert's period of residence at The Hospital was ending. Meeting with his parents for the last time, I told them that his place now was at home. He still had very serious conflicts and would require psychotherapy for many more years but not in a hospital setting: his need for confinement was over. He could no longer be protected from the world, but now he no longer needed to be protected from it.

CHAPTER EIGHT

John: The Boy Who Could Not Curse

He was blond, small, thin—and very frightened. "I was dying when I came here," John said. During his early weeks at The Hospital I learned of the horrifying sexual experiences which John had endured early in his life, experiences which, however, left him strangely innocent. Perhaps it was his religiosity which protected him against the full weight of these traumas and the darker impulses they aroused in him, that rage which continually threatened to overwhelm him.

"If there's no war the United States will last a long time but not forever," John said a few days after we met. "Russia is moving closer to the United States and in a few million years you'll be able to walk from my house in Florida to Russia: there'll be no Atlantic Ocean, only a Pacific Ocean. But God will last forever: God is super-powerful. If there's a Third World War, Jesus will send his angels and they'll stop it. Man has nuclear weapons and he discovered relativity but God gave man his brain and isn't capable of being harmed by nuclear weapons since God is supernatural. I've had a lot of problems in my life so the Lord sent me here [to The Hospital]." Later that week John spoke of those events which, early in his life, had predestined his need for treatment at The Hospital.

We never did learn what caused his grandfather's actions. Sometimes, John related them to his grandfather's wartime head injuries; other times he spoke of his grandfather's brutal childhood experiences. And I never met John's parents: they had died in an auto accident when John was four years old.

John had an older sister and a younger brother. When they were children, his grandfather sexually molested them, forcing John first to witness and later to participate in these events. The damage which these experiences did to John's mind was very great. He spoke of them in only a few of his therapy sessions, and this only during our earliest weeks of contact. He never spoke of them again. But he puzzled over the consequences of this and other of his grandparents' behavior for many years: the rages which caused his grandfather to destroy his wife's cherished antique glass collection and to kill John's pet lamb; and his grandmother's concern that he not be involved in "sinful" activities like going to the movies, dancing, or being assertive.

John grew to adolescence fearing closeness, fearing his feelings, fearing to assert himself, possessing a mind which had been shattered by the terrible experiences he endured as a child. Thus, being incapable of understanding and only little capable of controlling those feelings which coursed through him, John came to The Hospital and to my office facing the river, seeking aid lest he "die."

I spoke very little during John's early months of treatment. During one therapy session I spoke only two words: my response to his greeting, "Hello, John," were my only words during the time we spent together. His continuous ruminating monologue pervaded our contact and, at the end of that session, he said emphatically, "Our talk was very useful!" It was! Because *he* spoke. Like pus suppurating from a physical wound, John's speech relieved the internal psychological pressure dammed up from his years of unspoken fears and concerns.

During our early years of contact John began, very tentatively, to question his life, trying to determine why it became as it had and why he had become who he was. Why was he at The Hospital? Did this mean that he was crazy?

His grandfather's behavior was very crazy! Would he someday act like his grandfather? Why did he have problems? Because he had watched too much television or eaten too much ice cream as a child?

Absurd though some of John's conclusions were, the process which created them was helpful. Because mental processes develop through use, it was partially through his struggle to develop a theory of his existence within which his unusual life experiences could be explained that John's shattered mind was healed. This allowed him, eventually, to leave The Hospital and function independently, rather than to require lifetime care.

However, most of John's speech during those early years consisted not of self-questioning but of his continual description of daily events in his life: incidents on his ward, a new pair of shoes, the amusing remark of a teacher, the crazy behavior of another patient, the foods he liked and disliked. For three sessions weekly I listened, intervening only occasionally to add a remark designed to raise his self-esteem, or to strengthen his trust in his capacity to judge reality, or to increase his feeling that he was a worthwhile person.

Thinking back over those years, I sometimes wonder at my patience. There are few experiences more difficult than involuntary involvement in a repetitive activity. Perhaps this is why in classical mythology, Sisyphus, as punishment, was ordered by the Gods to live in Tartarus (a sunless abyss below Hades), and condemned forever to roll a stone to the top of a slope only to watch it fall and then to begin his task anew.

My task was easier for I understood that John's healing required that he speak compulsively and that I act as his friend and his helper,* listening to his description of the ordinary incidents in his daily life and thus saving him from "death."

John was a model patient. No patient in the history of The Hospital caused as little difficulty as he. When he was assigned chores, he did them. When a homework assignment was expected, his was produced on time. He never missed and was very rarely late for his therapy appointments. John was a dependable, courteous, decent, uncomplaining boy. For this reason he was, occasionally, used by The Hospital staff, designated as roommate to a patient whose behavior was as asocial as John's was exceptional.

It took years of treatment before John first requested a favor from a Hospital administrator. His request was refused! I no longer recall whether John discussed the incident with me, but I do remember the administrator telling me the sorrow he felt when he had to refuse the first request this uncomplaining boy had ever made of him: a six-week leave from The Hospital to visit his aunt in Louisiana. John was offered three weeks' leave but refused this. Thus John could allow himself to request his first favor only when it was likely to be refused.

John was unable to express anger. Even when another patient acted disgracefully toward him (as by urinating on the bathroom floor near his slippers while he was in the shower) John remained calm rather than give way to those feelings he so greatly feared.

*The four basic ways in which a psychotherapist relates to his patient ("psychotherapeutic postures") are described in Chapter 6.

Although an excellent athlete, John's performance was often mocked by the other patients who realized he would accept insults and aggressive acts rather than assert himself against them. In all the years which I knew John, I heard him curse only once. We were both in the same restaurant, several tables apart. He took out his wallet, began counting his money and, being accidentally jostled by a passing waiter, John dropped his change on the floor. He then uttered the strongest and only oath I ever heard him speak: "Oh my gosh!"

John was afraid of girls. A handsome boy, his attention was sought by many girls at The Hospital but his fear of closeness and sexuality caused him to "misunderstand" and thus to ignore their interest. Every Sunday he attended church with a local family. John, extremely courteous and likable, was soon regarded almost as a member of the family. He remained for Sunday dinner and "dropped in" during the week. Fifteen-year-old Kay was a member of this family. For several years John told me of his great love for this girl, of his plans for their eventual marriage. He wanted only a religious wife and Kay seemed a perfect choice: they were members of the same church and thought similarly about life. And she was very lovely—slim, with long blond hair. Thus did John's search for his mate seem ended.

John often spoke of how to ask Kay out, what words to use. He ruminated endlessly about where they could go on a date. Finally he revealed a startling fact: that he had never spoken to Kay. John was far more comfortable with the idea of being in love than with actually being in love, and with the thought of intimacy than its experience.

Soon John became involved in a religious youth group and described, with a mixture of pride and amazement, the activities he found himself involved in: joyriding in a convertible with the other teenagers and attending (very subdued) parties. But some months later he abandoned this group for he found himself becoming too involved in their activities and feared "to lose control."

Afraid of his inner strivings yet being compelled by his human nature to follow them, John's behavior often seemed puzzling to those who failed to realize his ambivalence about virtually all that he sought. One of John's most earnest endeavors was to learn how to meet girls. He often asked, "What can I talk about?" While his question largely reflected his ambivalence about closeness and discomfort over his status as a patient in a psychiatric hospital, it also reflected his continual desire to act proper and "normal," to use "the right method" to pick up a girl.

Believing that he would discover his own method of dealing with the situation when he was ready, I continually refused to advise him. Finally, in response to his entreaties, I suggested several general "techniques" I had found useful (as, sitting next to a woman in a restaurant and speaking about the food). The following week John reported his success. He had sat next to a girl in a restaurant and begun speaking with her. She was also a high school student, and lived about twenty miles from The Hospital. They spoke animatedly for a half hour and discussed meeting to see a film. It was only after she left that John realized he had neglected to obtain her last name or telephone number. But, he sighed, perhaps he would meet her again.

When John was admitted to The Hospital he had many fears, the most uncomfortable being that people were watching him as he walked in the street. Gradually, after years of treatment, his fears lessened and he began to explore, with increasing freedom, cities near The Hospital. Finally he made the big move! He traveled into Washington, D.C., by train. Thereafter, about once a month, John traveled into Washington to walk around and to buy books. He often talked about how dangerous the streets were but, thus far, nothing untoward had occurred. Arriving at work one Monday morning, I was asked by an attendant, "Did you hear about John's mugging this weekend?" Later that day John described his experience.

After purchasing books, he had walked along a major street, then into a poor neighborhood. The streets were relatively crowded. He noticed an unshaven, unsavory person in his fifties alongside him. John stared at him for several seconds and the man walked on. When the man was about fifteen feet ahead of him he turned and faced John. John stopped walking and the two stared at each other for several seconds. The man turned and walked on, stopping a few moments later. He walked back to where John was standing and, after stating that he had a gun in his pocket, asked John how much money he had. Within several moments John was robbed of $58, a significant part of his life savings. Then, shaken but unharmed, he returned to The Hospital.

John and I discussed this incident many times, finally concluding that by his behavior he had, most likely, brought about that incident which he most feared. His fear was not primarily of physical injury (although this, of course, existed) but that such an incident would unleash his rage and he might then, despite the great psychological barriers he had against acting violently, strike out and seriously injure another person. Thus John's meek demeanor and massive control over his spontaneity helped protect him from the unfortunate consequences which would arise were he to act upon the fear and rage he possessed.

But John was slow to recognize the degree to which, after several years of treatment, he had changed. To see that he was now capable of experiencing and acting upon feelings which would have devastated him had he been aware of them when he first entered The Hospital. No longer that same boy who, years earlier, had sought aid lest he "die," John had become an adult, forced to confront the decisions and difficulties which adults face: the choice of a mate, the choice of a vocation, and (or so we at The

Hospital thought) what to do when afflicted by venereal disease.

Despite his mature appearance John was, in many ways, still a child. He and a friend would often make animal noises in class and giggle. Having never been free enough as a child to allow himself to act silly, now, at seventeen, he occasionally acted like a five-year-old child. And John was terrified of intimacy. Thus it was with a sense of incredulity that I heard the internist's statement, "John might have VD." My response was brief: "That's impossible!" I said it was inconceivable that John, psychologically, at this point in his life, could tolerate sexual contact. The doctor listened. But, he said, he had all the classic symptoms: a genital discharge, itching, and discomfort during urination. The results of the tests would be known in a few days; meanwhile an appointment with a urologist was arranged for John the following week.

Despite our attempt to discuss other matters, John's "venereal disease" dominated his next few therapy sessions. And despite my absolute certainty of its impossibility, I did ask whether he had sexual contact: his response was a hesitant "no." But John's hesitancy did not indicate that he was lying for he did not lie. Rather, it was the manner in which he made any assertion or conducted any activity. (Thus he required 1½ hours to complete several figure drawings during a psychological evaluation, a task for which most adolescents required ten to fifteen minutes.)

This topic also crept into my occasional conversations with the internist: so persuasive was I that we both came to half-believe the "toilet-seat theory": that John's contact had been with an infected toilet seat rather than genital (a far more credible possibility for John but one far less plausible scientifically).

Finally, the results came. John did have a genital infection but not a venereal disease. Being uncircumcised, he should have washed beneath the foreskin of his penis when he showered but did not: he had never been told to do this. Probably his hesitancy to touch his genitals also weighed in this matter.

John had been at The Hospital for many years and had changed considerably. He had begun to be assertive and, tentatively, to speak to girls. He was a conscientious worker and an excellent student: he had held a part-time job at The Hospital since shortly after his admission, and he often stayed up studying until midnight. But he remained a loner, preferring to read in his room (biographies, books about Scandinavia) rather than to socialize. Often I had to intervene with well-meaning attendants when they tried to pressure him into joining group activities. "When he's ready to be with others, he will," I would say. "Leave him alone. And if he's never ready well, one doesn't have to be a 'groupie.' There are all manner of lives." My statement was rhetorical.

Within several months after I met John, I realized that he would never be a sociable person. He was a very courteous, very likable boy. I expected him to "come together," to change very slowly, but he would remain emotionally inhibited throughout his life. He would do well at school and thereafter be a dependable, conscientious worker. Very likely he would marry and, possibly, be dominated by his wife. And, most importantly, he would never be in a psychiatric hospital again.

These thoughts went through my mind during John's final months at The Hospital. Despite my reluctance to make decisions for him, I encouraged him to attend a school in a large city in Florida rather than the small, geographically isolated school in Louisiana which he preferred. I feared that the enforced social activities of the smaller school and the unavailability of psychotherapeutic treatment there would create too much pressure for him.

John followed my advice (which was also that of his grandmother and his high school adviser) and attended the school in Florida. Once he returned to The Hospital to visit. He was doing well in school and had dated a girl several times. He had begun to play tennis regularly and had joined a local church. He liked his new therapist: perhaps (he said wistfully) it was time for a change. Perhaps it was.

The emotional demands which treating John made upon me were very different from those I experienced with Robert and my other patients at The Hospital. While treating them I encountered frequent crises punctuated by brief periods of quiescence. With some (such as Robert) the crises were fewer and the periods of quiescence more extensive, but the same pattern existed, with each crisis presaging a major change in the way the adolescent related to their experience, each crisis anticipating a major period of growth.

I experienced no such crises while treating John. His psychological growth was slow and steady. He was the most trouble-free patient at the institution: completely trustworthy, extraordinarily conscientious and courteous, he had never caused problems like other patients— suddenly hitting another child on the head with a baseball bat as he sat quietly on a sofa in the hallway, or setting a fire which devastated several rooms and caused many thousands of dollars in damages, or putting glass fragments into a sugar bowl, or running naked into a girls' ward, or dealing in drugs, or threatening to poison the staff's food.

John was a godsend to The Hospital: apart from his need for psychotherapy, education, and a minimal degree of understanding, he made few demands on it, thus allowing the staff time to deal with those other almost daily crises which constantly threatened to disrupt the operation of the institution.

About a year before John's discharge I realized he had changed as much as he could at that point in his life. He could not be more than slightly spontaneous or tolerate more than very limited feelings. At times in that last year I pressured him, encouraged him to explore his thoughts, feelings, and experiences with slightly more depth and from a different perspective: his response was to change slightly, but then to become anxious and to resume his former behavior. And so, finally, I realized that in pressuring him I was trying to force him to live in accordance with my concept of a meaningful life rather than in accordance with his nature. And I stopped pressuring him and relaxed, and he relaxed, and continued developing at his own pace, toward his own goals.

CHAPTER NINE

Jim: The Psychotherapist Who Sought Love and Met Death

Draw near . . . The hour to lay bare
My secret to your eyes at last is here.
Mithridate (Act III)
Jean Baptiste Racine

Eva

When Eva entered The Hospital, she had to wear a corset to prevent her mutilating her breasts. Later this was no longer necessary, but other behavior still reflected her deep ambivalence at being a woman. She dressed boyishly, her clenched fists swinging at her sides as she walked. Her hair was often disheveled, her hands dirty, and her hair unbrushed. Her face showed pain and hurt and heavily controlled rage. Only her sensitive, delicate eyes revealed her femininity.

Eva was greatly feared by the other adolescents on her ward. She threatened and abused them unmercifully, relentlessly tearing at their weaknesses. Her hostility and rage and physical strength made her their leader, a position which she scrupulously defended. When her demands were ignored she acted in any manner to have her way: assaulting a patient, screaming, destroying property, or harming herself. Only warmth from a trusted staff member would assuage her fury, relieve that self-hatred which motivated so much of her behavior.

Jim came to The Hospital with an awesome reputation. Having successfully treated hospitalized adolescents with enormous creativity, he was destined to be a leading figure in treating patients and training staff. While all patients at The Hospital were difficult to treat, most being "graduates" of several other institutions, a few were considered particularly demanding. Many of these, including Eva, were assigned to Jim for treatment soon after he arrived.

Jim's reputation was not undeserved. He succeeded in establishing an intense relationship with several profoundly disturbed adolescents. One of these was Eva. I don't know what about her claimed his commitment. Certainly not her physical appearance for her loveliness became apparent only in later years. Nor could it have been her demeanor, for her continual hostility caused her to be liked by few at The Hospital. Jim's greatest success as a clinician had been with institutionalized adolescents who, although less regressed than Eva and his other patients at The Hospital, had been more greatly feared by society: one, the son of a famous American writer, had been hospitalized in lieu of imprisonment for criminal activities; another had murdered a playmate. Perhaps Jim sensed a similarity between their self-destructive activities and hers. Or perhaps it was the frustration he sensed beneath Eva's rage which attracted him and aroused in him that deep commitment which was so crucial to both their lives. We can never know. But something about her attracted his interest, aroused his empathy, and fostered his dedication to her healing.

Jim's behavior provoked anger among the staff. They felt that Eva's treatment took too much of his time, and they resented (or feared) his neglect of other duties. Or perhaps they were jealous of his preoccupation with her treatment, his ability to involve himself in his work to a greater extent than they could. Jim's commitment to Eva was open-ended. He gave her as much attention as she demanded, often spending two to three hours a day speaking with her, listening to her, nurturing her.

Recognizing her intense longing for the nurturing she never had, but in opposition to accepted clinical practice, Jim allowed her to sit in his lap and held her as they spoke. Over the years Eva's difficult behavior diminished and, for the first time, she became immersed in her education. She studied seven days a week, intent on repairing her academic deficiencies. Only during Jim's vacation was she incapable of maintaining her studies.

After several more years of treatment Eva was discharged from The Hospital and began working as a clerk in a store about forty-five miles away. Her good intelligence and capacity for leadership were soon recognized and she was made a supervisor, being granted responsibility for monitoring the work of several other employees. She began attending a university part-time in the evening, studying for a college degree. And she maintained her contact with Jim, occasionally meeting him for lunch or an outing. He was proud of her achievements and carried photographs of her in his wallet as a parent does of their child.

Jim

Mental health was the last profession one would have expected Jim to choose. His father had been a writer. Probably this was why Jim's first career was in publishing, his creativity gaining him, at an early age, a major business award. I often asked him why he left the glamour of a successful business career for the stress of the clinic. His response was always the same: "I wanted a life different from my father's." I never learned anything about Jim's mother for he never spoke of her.

I met Jim when he was in his late fifties. His vivacity and wit were impressive. His grayish white hair did not detract from his youthful appearance. Despite the more than twenty-five year difference in our ages, we soon became friends, often lunching together at The Hospital. It was he who informed me of the impending dismissal, because of hospital politics, of the chief psychiatrist, the person to whom I was closest during my initial years at The Hospital, and it was Jim who comforted me for my prospective loss. It was with him, too, that I shared my suspicions of the gravely unprofessional conduct of a staff member, the madness which appeared to be governing his "treatment" of a female patient. Jim listened quietly as I spoke. He promised to inform The Hospital's director of the matter but he never did. I no longer wonder why.

Jim was a very controlled man. When he was in his forties he developed cataracts in both eyes. An operation was performed: for it to be successful he had to remain motionless for days after the operation. Despite his active nature, Jim lay unmoving during this period, rejecting the tranquilizers which had been suggested by the surgeon. He related his early development of these cataracts to the blows to the head he had received while a boxing champion in the military.

Jim was a powerful man and well trained in the techniques of personal combat. Only occasionally did he lose control. Once, several years after the death of his wife, he had dinner with a former student. Upon leaving the restaurant, his companion noted several men following them. Dismissing her concern, he accompanied her the short distance to her home, leaving her at the door. Then, walking apparently aimlessly, he lured the men into a darkened, secluded alley. Several moments later Jim strode alone from the alley: his attackers lay bleeding on the ground.

Despite his clinical career, Jim maintained ties with his former business activities. He acted as consultant to a major European corporation, receiving for his services a high fee, occasional trips to Europe, and the use of an expensive sports car which, each year, was exchanged for a new model. Jim loved to drive. Finally, in what turned out to be the last year of his life, he personally purchased the exotic automobile which had been leased for him. I can still visualize him waving to me as he drove away from The Hospital.

I cannot conceive of Jim owning anything that was not the best. He wore a very expensive wristwatch but advised me against such a purchase. "They all tell the same time," he said. He vacationed at the most exclusive resorts and, as I said, he drove a very expensive sports car. Yet these purchases and vacations occurred in his later life, after the death of his wife. Whether he was the same man in his earlier life, I don't know. I didn't know him then. Perhaps his wife's death changed him even more greatly than I realize.

Jim's wife had a very strong will. All who met her have so described her. Her manner of death is evidence of this. Dying of cancer, she waited until Jim was absent and then ended her life. Some say that Jim knew of her plan, arranged for her to be alone, and provided her with the medication which would, finally, end her agony. Others spoke of her insistence that he attend a party, and of his returning home to find her dead. But are these details really important? I'm only sure that she was suffering terribly and that she died and that he needed her, for her strength of character gave a gravely needed stability to his life.

Jim changed following his wife's death. He no longer seemed as sure of himself as he had been. And his conversation became repetitive: often during lunch he would tell the same amusing story, at which we would laugh though more from affection for him than enjoyment.

And Jim's language became occasionally disconnected: he would phrase theoretical explanations which sounded brilliant but were, when examined closely, meaningless. But we liked him and cared for him and excused his increasing abruptness with patients and failed to question his long telephone conversations with his girl friend.

Six months before Jim's death he became interested in bicycling and determined that, like his other possessions, his bicycle had to be the best. After reading countless cycling magazines and books, he decided to purchase a custom manufactured bicycle in France. That summer, traveling to Paris with his girl friend, an editor at a publishing firm, he purchased two custom made bicycles, one for each of them. They rented a small van and drove through Europe, occasionally stopping to ride their new bicycles. After returning to America, Jim and his girl friend rode their bikes early each morning before work, passing along those lovely country roads near his home. It was during one of these rides that Jim died of a heart attack at the age of sixty-four

.

Eva and Jim

The day after Jim's death I asked The Hospital's director, "Did you locate Jim's girl friend?" "No," he said, "but we found his wife: Eva!" Her job, her attendance at the university, her independent life were all lies. Eva was so fearful of independence that she refused to allow Jim to open a bank account for her so she could obtain money without asking him. She spent her days cooking and cleaning their home, which she rarely left. They had married soon after her discharge from The Hospital. And, of course, his long daily telephone conversations had been with her, as was his trip to Paris.

Some had known: he had shared knowledge of their marriage with a few of his oldest friends. They were aghast at his violation of professional ethics and the forty-year difference in age between them. None at The Hospital knew. I remembered his saying to me, "I keep asking Eva to marry me." "What if she agrees?" I asked in surprise, disbelieving his statement, considering it to reflect the silliness through which clinicians occasionally relieve their tension. "Why, then, I'll marry her," he replied. Puzzled, I said nothing, not then realizing that he was seeking understanding for something that had already occurred. Jim finally did get from me the understanding he so greatly needed—but only after his death.

The funeral service was held in a large chapel in Washington. I arrived early and watched as the people arrived. Jim's colleagues were seated to the rear, Eva was in the first row, and the patients from The Hospital between.

Some of the patients Jim had been treating were sobbing. Others who had only limited contact with him were silent. The service was brief. The eulogy spoke of his years of professional service, of the children he had healed, of the adolescent who repeatedly fled the institution until Jim arranged for the boy to be given a job painting the fence around it, this task alleviating his ambivalence about treatment by permitting him to be simultaneously both inside and outside the institution. Of course Eva was not mentioned. Or his later years.

Jim was too knowledgeable a clinician not to have realized the damage that his intimacy with Eva had wrought. He knew that both intimacy and healing cannot exist simultaneously between patient and doctor. Jim's involvement with Eva had halted her psychological growth: it had precluded her from so changing that she might become an autonomous person and, eventually, choose a lover rather than become involved with a man to whom she was symbiotically tied as she had been, years before, to her parents who so damaged her. And then Jim died and Eva was set free to grow. But now, incapable of independence, she spent hours of the day seated outside yet another doctor's office, awaiting her daily treatment and desperately trying to avoid having to re-enter a hospital.

I think that Jim welcomed death. The guilt and lies in his life had grown too great, become unbearable. He had lied even to Eva's parents (who lived in a far-off state), telephoning them monthly to reassure them that Eva was doing well in her "psychotherapy treatment" with him. And so Jim exerted himself, continually increasing the distance of his long bicycle rides, seeking that deliverance which only death seemed able to provide him. He looked unwell in his final months: yet the results of numerous electrocardiograms were negative. But a sore on his mouth was healing poorly and I wondered why. And his behavior seemed too hurried, too frantic. And then he died.

How should we remember Jim? As a clinician who, bereft of the stability he had found in his relationship with his wife and desperate for comfort, sought it from a child in his care? Or as a man who was too greatly affected by his work? Several years before his death he confided to me that he found working with the very regressed patients at The Hospital too stressful, that he had changed since he began working there.

Or as a man who, in a moment of weakness, had allowed himself to become intimate with his patient. Then, consumed by guilt and fear and knowing that he could not regain the trust of his colleagues were knowledge of his behavior to become public, had continued the involvement with her, fearful that she would speak of their intimacy were it to end?

But perhaps the judgment of Jim's behavior, if one must be made, should be from another perspective—from that provided by Robert, the autistic boy. For it was gentle, compassionate Robert who, unconcerned with matters of ethics and psychopathology, saw Jim's behavior as perhaps it should be remembered and as, perhaps, Eva will remember it throughout her life. He said softly, "He must have loved her very much."

CHAPTER TEN

Farewell to The Hospital

The Boy Who Predicted His Father's Death

Some years ago an architect in his early forties contacted me for treatment. His first appointment was scheduled, as it happened, shortly before he was to enter a hospital for surgery which contained little risk and of which he professed small concern. At the initial meeting he spoke of an early life experience. One evening, seated in his father's lap, he said to him, "You're going to kill yourself." "Don't be silly," his father responded. That night his father died, purportedly from a heart attack. Fifteen years later this man suggested to his older sister that they have regular electrocardiograms since their father had died of a heart disorder. She responded, "No. He killed himself. You were told a lie to spare your feelings." The man felt nothing when she said this but four months later he began crying for the first time in his life. He spoke of this and other experiences: his marriage, his feeling for his child, his plan to begin a business of his own. He had never taken a vacation: the prospective four-day hospitalization was virtually his first absence from work since he graduated from college. When we spoke again after his operation, his behavior was very different. His psychological defenses were collapsing and he was rapidly becoming acutely psychotic. That week, while trying to arrange hospitalization for this seriously ill man, I had contact with him literally day and night, speaking with him for long periods even in the middle of the night.

I will probably remember this man for the rest of my life. Yet, although crises at The Hospital were almost always less stressful than this (for a hospital has built-in resources and support personnel for coping with life-threatening emergencies), my work there had a far greater effect on my life than did my concurrent private practice.

The Hospital was a place of refuge for the adolescents who came there for treatment. Their situation was poignant: this was their last opportunity to change their lives—and they knew it!

Sometimes after years of treatment a patient achieved their intellectual and emotional potential, and sometimes significant psychological damage remained. Even those infrequent amusing incidents that entered my work did little to conceal the tragic psychological deformities which produced them. It is some of these memories which I now carry with me that are described in this chapter.

The Girl Who Feared Love But Gave Me a Wedding Ring

She was a very sexy girl—and very disturbed. Often she came to my office with her wrists swathed in bandages which concealed the cuts she had made during the night. She was terrified of closeness but, sensing her need for it, simultaneously sought and rejected it. And mistaking sexuality for closeness, she glided through The Hospital offering her lush body as if it were ripe for pleasure rather than barricaded by multitudinous conflicts. I'll never forget the day she sat in my office, showed me a piece of glass with which she planned to cut her wrists that night, then dropped it down her blouse, partially desiring me to take it from her bosom.

After her early months of treatment, such behavior became exceptional. Usually she spoke softly of her life: her difficulty in expressing anger; her fear of the rage which erupted periodically from her father; her symbiotic, childlike, imprisoning attachment to her parents. As she began to trust me and to share her most private thoughts and feelings, she also began to dress more seductively: her sweaters and blouses grew tighter and her skirts even briefer than they had been. She became afraid to enter my office, fearful of the healing she was experiencing, fearful that she would be destroyed were she to act out her growing desires to be assertive and to experience intimacy, fearful that my control over my behavior might not be greater than hers. Gradually she came less frequently to her scheduled therapy sessions and was increasingly hostile to me when we passed in the hall.

After several months I cornered her in the hallway and led her to my office. There, I again suggested that she be transferred to a female therapist and asked her feelings on the matter. In contrast to her previous vehement rejection of this suggestion she now said, "It would be OK."

So I hadn't seen her for several months on that day she dropped into my office. She hurriedly gave me a ring shaped like a wedding band which she had made in a metalworking class, and then slipped away. A week later she placed a note under the door of my office. It read, "Loving means trying to understand why people do the things they do."

The Boy Who Shot Himself in the Leg

My first encounter with Bill seemed unpromising: he was roaring angry and kicking in the glass panels on a door near the staff dining room.

Bill first received psychological treatment at the age of eight when he was taken to a local hospital after he shot himself in the leg with his father's revolver. His behavior during his brief stay on the pediatric ward was so unusual that a referral to the mental health clinic was made. Thereafter Bill frequented various clinics and was eventually hospitalized at several institutions beginning in his early adolescence. At eighteen years of age he entered The Hospital, profoundly depressed, deeply self-destructive, possessing the degree of anger which was appropriate to one who had such marked conflicts and frustrations as he had.

Bill was not a likable person. His usual greeting was to thrust his fist three inches from my face and curse my "stupidity" and "craziness." His fury was particularly great on those mornings after he had experienced a sexual dream for Bill was terrified of intimacy. He was a difficult boy to interact with: once, in anger, he smashed a pie on the head of a staff worker; and he was virtually impossible to awaken in the morning. But he was liked by several attendants: they sensed the pain he was experiencing and the naiveté beneath his powerful, adult physique.

After several years of therapy Bill's behavior improved: now only rarely did he threaten a staff worker or destroy property. But his control over his behavior was fragile: he was one of the very few patients I treated who regularly required tranquilizing medication to be maintained at The Hospital.

Although a bright boy, it was impossible to involve Bill in school for more than several days at a time: fearing that he would harm another person, he would flee from the classroom when he experienced the least frustration. He began a vocational training program in electrical repair but left this too when, one afternoon, he feared that he would harm a teacher who had corrected his errors.

Despite his seething fury, Bill was often good-natured. He always spontaneously shared his French fried onions and potatoes on those frequent occasions when I drove him out of The Hospital for lunch. I learned, early in my contact with him, that the best way to remove him from a troubling situation on the ward was to take him out to eat. And he frequently spoke of taking me out to eat, of buying me a steak dinner after he left The Hospital and began working.

I began treating Bill late in my career at The Hospital, aware that it was likely I would leave before him, and that he would sting from my rejection as he had from those of his parents. Perhaps it was my feeling of guilt which caused me to buy him lunch on so many days during my last weeks at The Hospital.

I tried to involve him in yet another vocational training program before I left, hoping that he could make some degree of commitment to an independent, non-institutional life, that life which he felt so little deserving of. Immediately after his visit to that training program I sought a restaurant to alleviate the marked anxiety his interview had aroused. On our return to The Hospital I realized for the first time how greatly threatened he was by non-institutional life, and how dim his future was. I lunched with him on my last day at The Hospital, knowing that I could not do less and feeling guilty that I could not do more.

Paula

Paula was not an appealing girl. Her clothes were often filthy, and her blond hair was matted. While she stood with her fingers picking at the skin of her hands, her body shaking, we began speaking about her life. The numerous hospitalizations which she experienced since the age of seven; her sexual abuse by the older patients; her entrance into The Hospital as a teenager.

Her major desire was a simple one: that I act as had her recently deceased father, taking her shopping and to art galleries. She now engaged in some of these activities with her mother, a woman so disruptive that she was forbidden to visit The Hospital at all and met Paula at the train station in Washington for her periodic visits with her.

Once, before this edict, during an evening visit to The Hospital, being unable to find her way back to my office from the bathroom, Paula's mother pulled the fire alarm, causing the patients to flee the building into the snow, some still dressed in their pajamas. She often telephoned The Hospital's director at his home in the early hours of the morning (because she was unable to obtain my telephone number). When I asked him why he tolerated these intrusions into his personal life, his answer was brief: "She'd cause more problems if I didn't!"

The troubles she caused were not minor. Paula was very difficult to awaken: she was so unhappy that she preferred sleep far more than to be aroused and become aware of the emptiness of her life. Once a new attendant, frustrated at Paula's refusal to leave her room three hours after breakfast time, pulled her from her bed. Paula fell on the floor and bruised her arm. Her mother, noting the bruise, filed child abuse charges against the attendant and The Hospital. Shortly thereafter a government inspector arrived to investigate these charges. He read Paula's hospital record, then discussed the incident with the attendant and with me. Finally he spoke, alone, with Paula. After some discussion he indicated to Paula that he had no further questions and the girl rose to leave the office. The inspector, being unaware that patients were usually allowed to walk freely about The Hospital, attempted to restrain her until an attendant could be called to accompany Paula back to her ward. As soon as the inspector's hand touched her arm, Paula began shouting in a voice that echoed down the hall, "Help! Help! He's assaulting me!" It took many minutes of reassurance before the inspector regained his poise. His glowing report absolved The Hospital of any blame.

Paula, too, was a patient assigned to me late in my career at The Hospital. After many months of treatment the shaking of her body ceased, and instead of her previous continual recitation of the inadequacies of the staff she began speaking of her more private concerns: her rejection by other patients, her desire for a job, and her love for a doctor she had met at another hospital.

On several occasions when I answered her questions (for example, as to why she didn't have friends) with a statement which I knew would hurt her but which could not be withheld lest her life remain unchanged, she threatened to throw her cup of hot coffee in my face, but she never did.

No longer profoundly depressed and believing her life to be incapable of change, Paula began attending school and, for the first time in her life, accepted a part-time job at The Hospital, at which she worked like one possessed.

I treated her at least once daily during that period. And then I left her for my period at The Hospital had ended and I hoped that the end of her period there had begun. I hoped that she could continue her progress with another therapist but was unsure.

I remembered an older colleague who, before leaving an eminent treatment setting, had divided the severely disturbed children he was treating into three categories: those who had progressed enough to be safely transferred to another therapist, those who had not yet established a sufficiently strong relationship with him and thus could also be safely transferred, and those who were in the middle of their treatment and clinging desperately to his presence.

Only one boy fitted into the last category. My colleague left the institution (for he had pressing family matters: a handicapped child who required specialized education which was only available elsewhere) and became the clinical director of another facility.

Several years later he returned to the institution and met this child who, by his behavior, indicated that his former doctor would never be forgiven. The child would never allow his life to improve: he would remain in the institution always, existing there as a monument to his therapist's "betrayal," his "desertion" when he was most needed.

The doctor left the child and acted as he felt he had to: he got drunk and remained that way for several days. Then he left the institution, never to return.

And so I left Paula because I too had to leave. But I wondered about how her life would evolve. And I never saw her again.

I was friendly with many colleagues at The Hospital but intimate with few. There were few social gatherings and at these we spoke, naturally enough, about our work: the continual stress of treating such disturbed patients as were at The Hospital caused us, seeking catharsis, to discuss our work whenever we met. I had once tried without success to establish regular Friday afternoon cocktail parties: the only established social occasion remained the yearly Christmas party. But in response to my entreaties (and the concurrent desire of The Hospital's director) we occasionally had that cocktail party which I so earnestly sought. On those afternoons, at 4:00 P.M., the entranceway to the treatment section was locked and the director unlocked the cabinet nearest his desk. This cabinet was always sealed for its contents were confidential: a case of whiskey and innumerable jars of peanuts and packages of potato chips. It was during one of these cocktail parties that I learned from a colleague the following story.

The Mobster's Daughter Who Studied Psychology

Living in a prosperous suburban area, my colleague had grown friendly with many of his neighbors, several of whom were, reportedly, heavily involved in organized criminal activities. His wife had a flair for decorating and, having helped one of these neighbors decorate his home, received an invitation, along with her husband, to a party held in a penthouse apartment high above the streets of a great American city. Arriving at the apartment, they found a four-piece band, tables filled with the most expensive delicacies, and seven or eight other couples. All of the men present were married but none (except my colleague) was accompanied by his wife.

After several hours of drinking, a man, learning that my colleague was a child clinician, began speaking with some distress about his daughter. She was a brilliant student at an Ivy League college and wanted to become a child psychologist and to treat disturbed children. What was wrong with her? She should get married and have children and not be interested in such work. He had brought her up to be a credit to her family and now look how she acted. With these sad words, his drink drooped from his hand. My colleague, unable to comfort him, listened with a grave expression on his face until the unhappy man left him and drifted shakily toward the bar.

An Attempted Murder

He was awakened by the heat on his legs from the flames but could not move. The fire alarms were sounding and the room was wreathed in smoke. His roommate had fled and, as he heard the pounding of the attendants' footsteps in the hall, he too tried to flee but felt paralyzed, repetitive thoughts jumbling through his mind. Finally an attendant braved the smoke and dragged him from his bed as the noise of the fire engines was heard in the distance.

He had been raised in a family that provided little caring and much physical abuse. His "misdeeds" (as, opening a window) were punished by beatings. Once his mother, bandaging an injured finger, had warned him not to inform his father of this ministration. Growing up with parents who provided him with little more than neglect and madness, he had eventually been admitted to The Hospital where his well-developed ability to build psychological defenses against his very serious emotional conflicts enabled him to "come together" rapidly. Soon he became an excellent student at the school on the grounds of The Hospital, receiving his high school diploma, despite his severe emotional difficulties, at the usual age for adolescents. But these psychological defenses which enabled him to "come together" so quickly, his ability to develop obsessive thoughts to forestall thinking of thoughts and feelings he found painful, also inhibited his spontaneity. Thus he could not move rapidly even when, in danger of being burnt alive, he lay under the covers of his smoldering bed, thinking those repetitive thoughts which, though helpful to him in the past, now seemed to mandate his doom.

What had caused this murderous attack? A patient was angry with him though the grievance was uncertain. Even he who set the fire could not provide an adequate rationale for the deed. Perhaps it reflected a displacement of his angry feelings toward his parents or his therapist onto this boy. No one was sure.

Farewell to The Hospital:
Of Stanley and Robert and John and Jim

She came to my office and, appearing distressed, asked to speak with me. I invited her to sit down as I had on several previous occasions when, despite her being a patient assigned to another clinician, she had "dropped in." "I've heard that you're leaving," she said. "Is it because you feel uncomfortable about the things you told me about your life? I won't tell anyone."

Hearing these words, I felt moved as I had so often been during my years at The Hospital when I sensed the deep compassion of these patients whose lives were so devastated.

"No," I answered. "Those things I told you about my life I felt comfortable telling you. There are some matters I wouldn't feel comfortable sharing and those I didn't. I've been working here for many years and now it's time for me to leave."

She looked relieved and our conversation turned to other matters: her progress in school and the training required to become a psychologist. And when she left, seated alone in my office on my final day at The Hospital, I realized that a part of my life was ended.

During my stressful years at The Hospital I had learned a simple truth: that one must simultaneously war against their limitations, recognize their nature, and strive for love. Robert, the autistic boy, had believed in Jesus and sought everlasting love. John too had sought love. And Jim was destroyed by his search for love. And each had lived his life as he was bound to; each sought love as if that would provide their ultimate healing, as perhaps it does.

And so I come to the end of my tale: the stories of Robert and John and Jim, and Stanley, for on these pages is written my story too, and those of some of my patients who entrusted me with their lives, and those of some colleagues who permitted me to share their lives, all locked forever in my memory.

Once, walking near my office in New York City, far from that hospital where these events occurred, I saw an older man with grayish white hair. Hurriedly I caught up with him, knowing all the while that he could not be Jim. As indeed he was not. And of Robert and Mr. Giraffe: I have never seen them again.

CHAPTER ELEVEN

*The Unceasing Task of the Psychotherapist**

What can happen after psychotherapy ends are not the common attributes of friendship such as sharing meals, for such are forbidden to psychotherapists by their professional code. Instead, that more rare and valuable experience: realizing the accurate nature of the other and what really happened in their relationship. Misunderstood communications which were resolved, or not. Frailties and fears being spoken of, or remaining hidden.

Interpretations during psychotherapy must occur within a relationship during which a deep understanding of feelings and longings exist for only through this can a person's sense of self—their personality—be transformed, and their openness to new, healthier, and more fulfilling experiences occur.**

*Adapted from Goldstein, Stanley, 2011, *Shopping For A Shrink: Finding the Right Psychotherapist For You or Your Child,* Warwick, NY: Wyston Books, Inc., *chapter 30.*
**Atwood, G.E., & Stolorow, R.D., 1984, *Structures of Subjectivity: Explorations in psychoanalytic phenomenology.* Hillsdale, NJ: Analytic Press.

This is particularly important for those who experienced severe emotional derailments in childhood. Thereafter, they will be prone to anxiety and depression, and tend to be easily led by others. Their inaccurate perceptions and poorly articulated feelings may even result in medical problems: headaches, skin conditions, an immune disorder, or worse.

Through therapy, the tapestry of life becomes rewoven: nightmares disappear, and trauma linger as only faint memories. But therapy is not magic. Each person solves their problems as best they can, each process of life remains individual.

Freud advised that therapy can grant not happiness but only the gift of experiencing ordinary misery as life becomes simpler, unhindered by powerful, unconscious motives. By gaining better control over these, a person becomes more open to experiences and more likely to fulfill their needs.

Stacy,
as Child and Woman

I first treated Stacy for several years, after the death of her twin brother when she was five years old. Later, as an adolescent, she returned to therapy when she dropped out of high school. Stacy was a highly intelligent girl who struggled with an abusive alcoholic father but had a dedicated mother for support. Stacy returned to school, battled her problems, and was days from graduating—until a teacher insisted that she had failed to hand in an assignment and could not graduate. Stacy and her mother pleaded with the teacher, and her mother appealed to the principal and the school superintendent. But they held firm and the teacher wouldn't budge. Stacy became very depressed, went home, and cried.

But her mother had not given up. That next day, Friday, she returned to the school and again argued with the principal and school superintendent, losing her voice in the process. Finally, they relented: Stacy could graduate with her class if she handed in the missing report on Monday.

Stacy worked all weekend and handed in the assignment. Then she ran to the stadium where her class was practicing the graduation ceremony. When they saw her, knowing of her suffering, practice stopped while all three hundred students spontaneously chanted "Stacy Stacy Stacy" and teachers began crying. When Stacy's mother told me this story, my eyes were wet too.

Stacy got a part-time job at which she worked faithfully; and attended college with increasing commitment while going from bad boyfriends to better ones. Just before her twenty-third birthday I heard that she had given birth to a girl, an event which pleased both she and her husband who earlier seemed not to have been a good choice. But, Stacy's mother reflected, he loved her deeply and had been driven nearly crazy by her daughter's difficult behavior. Which we struggled with too.

Stacy's ambition, she once told me, was to use up her body by the time she was old. Or, in the words of Dylan Thomas, "Do not go gentle into that good night. Rage, rage against the dying of the light."

Therapists deal with the "real dark night of the soul...(when)...it is always three o'clock in the morning."*

*F. Scott Fitzgerald

They explore issues of shame and guilt, innocence and awareness, failure and triumph, pain and loss. Including the great questions: Why has my life become as it is? How much can it change? Or, more simply, why me?

Answers which can only come in time for they first need to be lived. Through life the answers may come, or not, and a crucial task of the psychotherapist is to encourage hope. The conviction that, despite despair and disappointment, strength exists and can prevail.

"Tho' much is taken, much abides...heroic hearts, Made weak by time and fate, but strong in will."*

Thus, above all, the psychotherapist must foster the patient's expectation that they will achieve a brighter dawn: that "the darkness shall be the light, and the stillness the dancing."**

*Tennyson, *Ulysses*
**T.S. Eliot, *East Coker*

APPENDIX

Confessions of Mrs. Malaprop:*
An Informal Glossary of
Selected Psychological Terms
Often Used Incorrectly

ANXIETY: See Chapter One.

AUTISM, INFANTILE: A most profoundly disturbing psychological disorder of young children. Symptoms include extreme isolation, the inability to communicate meaningfully with others, many language disturbances (as, echolalia—repeating words or phrases), and highly repetitive play.

BEHAVIOR MODIFICATION: Both a theory of human nature and a method of treatment for human psychological difficulties deriving from this theory. A child's behavior is viewed as evolving passively from their environment's actions upon them. Behavior which is rewarded is maintained; that which is not rewarded, or is punished, disappears. Other mechanisms, such as imitation and identification, are also viewed by some who espouse this theory as being important in determining how a child behaves. Treatment consists of the "reward" (usually through praise or attention) of "healthy" behavior and the "punishment" (by causing unpleasant events to be associated with it) of "unhealthy" behavior. Both psychoanalytically oriented and behaviorally oriented therapists use "rewards" and "punishments," but the former view this technique as but one minor aspect of treatment, while the latter view it as central to treatment.

*A character in a play by Richard Sheridan, *The Rivals* (1775), noted for her misuse of words.

CRAZY: An informal term, used to describe anything from inexplicable speech or behavior to an activity about which one feels passionately. Often used by adolescents to describe a statement or action which they find upsetting.

FREE ASSOCIATION: A technique used in traditional psychoanalytical treatment. The patient speaks all thoughts which enter their mind without, to the degree possible, restraint or censorship. This technique, as a major tool of treatment, is useful with only a very small and select group of patients. (See the discussion on psychotherapeutic postures in Chapter Six.)

HYSTERIA: A psychological disturbance in which there is a massive splitting off of psychological and physical functions, the major defense against discomfort being repression. Physical symptoms may include paralysis (such as the inability to move an arm) or blindness; psychological symptoms may include violent emotional outbursts and the loss of memory.

INSANE: A most complex legal term best left unused by lay people. Essentially it represents the attempt of the legal profession to allow an escape hatch in judicial action: its humane rejection of the concept that *all* people have total responsibility for their actions and are thus deserving of punishment. Who is not responsible for their actions? That person who is "insane" which means, according to judicial decisions in varying localities, that they are incapable of understanding either the nature of their act or that it was wrong (M'Naghten decision), or that they had no control over their behavior (irresistible impulse test), or that their act resulted from a mental disorder or disease (Durham decision).

INTELLIGENCE TEST: A psychological test used to measure those behaviors which psychologists consider to be "intelligent," as judgment, the ability to learn, the ability to adjust to changing circumstances, and the ability to think abstractly. These tests assume that all who take them share a common geographical and cultural environment. Thus an intelligence test devised for use with children in Great Britain cannot be used, unchanged, with American children. Intelligence tests which are administered individually (as, the Wechsler Intelligence Scale for Children, The Stanford-Binet) provide the most accurate results. During the analysis of the child's (or adult's) performance, each of their responses is examined to determine whether an emotional or neurological impairment is present and, if so, the approximate level of ability the child would be capable of were they to not suffer this limitation. Thus the determination of the IQ (or Intelligence Quotient) is by no means the only important data obtained. Interestingly, one of Jean Piaget's jobs, soon after receiving his doctorate, was to administer intelligence tests in Binet's laboratory in Paris. His interest in how children arrived at their *incorrect* responses pointed the way toward his lifetime study: how a child's thought develops.

NERVOUS BREAKDOWN: An informal term. When a marked change occurs in a person's life, this producing stress too great for them to tolerate, certain physical and psychological changes may occur: feelings of weakness and exhaustion, headaches, nausea, and diarrhea. These represent a reaction to psychological stress rather than a physical disorder. Although these symptoms are frightening they are helpful, for they cause the individual to change their life situation and/or seek aid, thereby alleviating the stress that was harming their psychological structure.

NEUROSIS: See Chapter Six.

OBSESSION: An involuntary, recurring thought accompanied by an emotional state (for example, sadness or anger). An obsession may be contrasted with a phobia, which is an involuntary fear of an object or circumstance in which the accompanying emotion is always very great anxiety.

PARANOIA: An ancient term, deriving from the Greek, meaning madness. A psychological disturbance distinguished by the holding of false, grandiose beliefs without an accompanying deterioration in intellectual capacity or inappropriate behavior and emotional responses in matters unrelated to the grandiose belief.

PSYCHOANALYSIS: A noun meaning three things: a method of investigating human behavior using the clinical techniques devised by Sigmund Freud (free association, dream interpretation, and the interpretation of resistance and transference phenomena); a method of treatment using these techniques; and a group of psychological theories about human behavior which have been derived from clinical experience and validated by this and other methods.

There is a belief that four to five sessions weekly of psychoanalytic psychotherapy is the most effective method of treatment for all psychological difficulties, that it is, so to speak, the "Cadillac" of treatment. This is untrue. I have treated patients both on a daily basis (and even twice daily in a hospital) and on a once or twice weekly basis (my usual frequency of treatment) and have seen changes using both. The optimal frequency of treatment (excluding financial considerations) depends very much on the difficulty. Too frequent treatment may even be harmful, precipitating rather than forestalling the occurrence of a psychosis in a person whose personality structure is fragile.

PSYCHOLOGICAL TEST: A means of gaining accurate information about a person to aid in formulating a decision. Thus an individual is asked certain questions, and their answers are compared to those given by others of similar cultural background, scores being determined by comparing the individual's performance with those of these others (the "normative group"). Psychological tests, when used for clinical purposes, are most often administered individually. Some, such as the various intelligence tests (the Wechsler Intelligence Scale for Children, the Stanford-Binet) and personality tests (the Rorschach Test) can provide extremely revealing insights into a person's intellectual and emotional nature.

PSYCHOSIS: See Chapter Six.

PUNISHMENT: Used in behavior modification theory to refer to any action which decreases the probability of a person or animal acting in some way. For example, if spanking a child after they run into the street decreases the probability that they will again act in this way, then spanking acts as a punishment for this behavior. If, however, the spanking does not reduce the probability that the child will run into the street, then, technically, no matter how painful the spanking, it is not a punishment for the act. Unfortunately corporal punishment, even if ineffective, tends to be used again for its use is rewarding to the parent! By alleviating *their* rage, it makes them feel better.

REINFORCEMENT (REWARD): Used in behavior modification theory to refer to any action which increases the probability of a person or animal acting in some way. For example, if the promise of a piece of candy causes a child's behavior to improve, candy may be said to reinforce their good behavior. The problem with a theory of human behavior which considers external reinforcements (money, food, attention, and the like) as crucial to human development is that it ignores other aspects of human nature: that children engage in play because it satisfies their curiosity and the development of their mind, and the altruism of older children and the love of adults. Interestingly, programmed school instruction (which utilizes immediate reinforcement) is most effective with intellectually limited individuals, probably because this method so simplifies their learning task that they can easily associate the significant elements they encounter. Programmed instruction is least satisfying to bright students.

REPRESSION: A term deriving from and basic to psychoanalytic thought and treatment. It describes the hypothesis that a person can, without awareness, banish from their mind (render unconscious) those actions, thoughts, and feelings which they find too painful or fear to acknowledge. Repression may be contrasted with *suppression* which is a deliberate, *conscious* attempt to forget a troubling thought or feeling.

RESISTANCE: A term deriving from psychoanalytic treatment which describes any speech or behavior of a patient which tends to forestall their becoming aware of the motivation underlying their behavior.

RORSCHACH TEST: A psychological test used to gain information about intellectual and emotional processes. It consists of ten plates containing unstructured forms, "inkblots." The subject is asked to describe what each blot reminds them of, their responses being recorded verbatim by the psychologist. Each response is scored according to three criteria: the *location* of the response (whether the whole blot or only part of it is used, and other factors); the *determinants* (whether the response concerns the form or color of the blot, and other factors); and the *content* of the response (whether a human figure, animal, or the like is seen). Interpretation of the responses to this test is most complex, and several years of training are required before a minimal, adequate level of proficiency is attained.

SCHIZOPHRENIA: A group of psychological disorders (psychoses) named by Eugen Bleuler in 1911 after what he regarded as their most significant feature: the "splitting" of parts of the mind which then begin to act independently. An example is when a person's whole life becomes motivated by an irrational thought.

Characteristic symptoms include limitations in the following ego capacities: the ability to judge the reality of events, self-awareness, memory, thinking, feeling, and the ability to contain anxiety. Can schizophrenia be healed? Usually, providing that appropriate and extensive treatment is made available. Probably the major difference for a psychotherapist between treating neurotic and treating psychotic disorders is that with the latter the therapist must work a little harder and worry a little more.

STIMULUS: Anything which incites action, thought, or feeling in a person.

SYMPTOM: See Chapter Four.

TRANSFERENCE: The attribution of feelings and attitudes from one experience onto another. One major task of psychoanalytically oriented psychotherapy is a reduction in the frequency of transference reactions which, because they derive from and are appropriate to earlier life experience, forestall further personality growth.

UNCONSCIOUS: A word used both as a noun and as an adjective. When used as a noun it refers to a part of the mind, *the unconscious*, consisting of those mental contents of which the person cannot become aware, as compared with *the conscious* which consists of those thoughts of which they are aware, and *the preconscious* which consists of those thoughts of which they can easily, merely by the act of attending, become aware. When used as an adjective it refers to a person's inability to be aware of or to participate in events surrounding them.

Dr. Stanley Goldstein is an author and psychologist who has appeared on national broadcasts including The Larry King Show and CourtTV. He lives in New York's Hudson Valley.